Advance Praise for *Money on the Table*

"Companies that do not embrace the benefits of a gender-balanced executive team, no matter how successful they may seem today, will fail to thrive tomorrow unless they integrate female problem-solving with the male problem-solving mentality that currently dominates. *Money on the Table* makes an excellent guide. Outstanding advice that will transform your organization and position it for enduring success!"

—**Marshall Goldsmith, The Thinkers50 #1 Leadership Thinker in the World.**

"*Money on the Table* does a great job of capturing the real issues of not having gender balance in leadership and exposes the criticality of solving this problem. Melissa's research, along with her work sharing the perspectives of a strong cross-section of executives and their experiences, helps us all better understand not only the realities of the challenges, but also what we can do about them. *Money on the Table* provides a complete picture of how businesses should be taking action to deal with those challenges. This is a must-read for every CEO."

—**Glenn Lyon, Chairman, and former Chief Executive Officer, The Finish Line, Inc.**

"In *Money on the Table*, Greenwell integrates insights from her many years' experience with qualitative research and science about bringing gender balance to companies. She creates a compelling case not only for why gender balance is important, but also how to achieve it. Those in leadership positions will find the ideas enlightening, implementable, and insightful for creating company value. We have seen firsthand how Greenwell's insights empower both women and men managers. It is important today that businesses not only identify their most talented employees, but value their diversity and arm them to create success for the company."

—**M. Kim Saxton, Clinical Associate Professor of Marketing, Indiana University Kelley School of Business**
—**Todd Saxton, Associate Professor of Strategy and Entrepreneurship, and Indiana Venture Fellow, Indiana University Kelley School of Business**

"Melissa's extraordinary experience in many male-dominated industries acts as a terrific foundation for preparing women and men to examine not only the causes of gender imbalances today, but also the actions we can take to make a real difference. Melissa's chapter titled 'My Story' sets the stage and allows us to truly appreciate her unique career journey, as well as the tremendous expertise and insights she shares throughout this book. The balance Melissa achieves by speaking to both women and men is refreshing and will encourage all of us to take action to build gender-balanced leadership. Thank you, Melissa, for creating such a practical and transformational resource for today's women and men. Your timing is perfect!"

—**Frank Costanzo, Senior Vice President, Caliper Corporation**

"The time has come to change how organizations are approaching gender diversity and *Money on the Table* is the catalyst for that change. This is a must-read for all leaders and diversity professionals to really understand why having a gender-balanced workforce is critical and how to go about making it happen. Melissa Greenwell understands what is needed and has outlined not only the business case, but also actionable steps. Don't just read it—learn from it and put the steps in motion!"

—**Alison Martin-Books, Founder of the Pass the Torch for Women Foundation and CEO of Diverse Talent Strategies**

MONEY

ON THE

TABLE

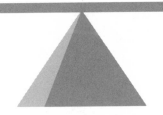

MONEY

ON THE

TABLE

HOW TO INCREASE PROFITS THROUGH
GENDER-BALANCED LEADERSHIP

MELISSA GREENWELL

GREENLEAF
BOOK GROUP PRESS

This publication is designed to provide accurate and authoritative information in regard to the subject matter covered. It is sold with the understanding that the publisher and author are not engaged in rendering legal, accounting, or other professional services. If legal advice or other expert assistance is required, the services of a competent professional should be sought.

Published by Greenleaf Book Group Press
Austin, Texas
www.gbgpress.com

Distributed by Greenleaf Book Group

For ordering information or special discounts for bulk purchases, please contact Greenleaf Book Group at PO Box 91869, Austin, TX 78709, 512.891.6100.

Design and composition by Greenleaf Book Group and Kim Lance
Cover design by Greenleaf Book Group and Kim Lance

Cataloging-in-Publication data is available.

Print ISBN: 978-1-62634-369-6

eBook ISBN: 978-1-62634-370-2

Part of the Tree Neutral® program, which offsets the number of trees consumed in the production and printing of this book by taking proactive steps, such as planting trees in direct proportion to the number of trees used: www.treeneutral.com

TreeNeutral®

Printed in the United States of America on acid-free paper

16 17 18 19 20 21   10 9 8 7 6 5 4 3 2 1

First Edition

My memory has a library filled with sound bites from leaders both past and present—people who mentored me and paved a path for my career. They are now joined by those who contributed to my research for this book and by others who gave me advice or graciously connected me to resources. When I think about all of them, I don't think about their relation to their profession, the companies they have worked for, or their titles. I think about what they stand for and what they mean to others. They give back and prop up the people around them, simply in exchange for the privilege of leading. That is their legacy—not just leading, but mentoring.

To all leaders who mentored me in some way and to mentors everywhere, I dedicate this book to you.

CONTENTS

PROLOGUE

DURING MOST OF MY NEARLY THIRTY YEARS IN CORPO-
rate America, working with public and private companies of
all sizes and industries, I've held a senior leadership role—had
a "seat at the table," surrounded almost exclusively by men.
Until recently, I didn't spend time thinking about how I got
there or why I was most often the only female. Instead, I
stayed focused on the daily challenges of running the business. I didn't think about why other women should be there,
how I might help, or what we might be missing, as a business,
by not having more women at the table.

> **While the global population is
> largely gender balanced, men hold
> eighty-five percent of senior leadership
> positions in public companies.**

Now that I reflect on this subject, I realize I'm not alone.
I have become part of a broader movement to help women

across the globe earn positions of leadership and succeed in them. Many countries around the world, led by several in Europe, are taking steps to get more women in senior leadership roles and on company boards. In almost every city in America, women's leadership and mentoring organizations are on the rise in existence and in participation. Universities are creating leadership initiatives specifically for women. We see it in the entrepreneurial community, as private equity funds are being created by women for the funding of women-owned businesses and start-ups. And thanks in part to *Lean In* author and Facebook COO Sheryl Sandberg, more women in senior leadership are taking a stronger, more active role in supporting the professional development of their female counterparts. It's time to seize this momentum.

In conference after conference, panel after panel, book after book, and article after article, women *and* men are speaking up loudly and more frequently about the lack of female talent in senior positions, ranging from business and health care to education and government. The statistics are updated and regurgitated ad nauseam: Only twenty-three Fortune 500 companies are led by women, only nineteen percent of public board seats are held by women, only fifteen percent of senior leadership roles are filled by women, and so on. In spite of this issue being in the spotlight, we're barely moving the needle. We need to actively build and keep our pipeline of female talent and to have more women in senior and executive positions.

The talents that women bring to the business world fit well with its changing demographics. The most common age in the United States is twenty-two, and the generation that will take our place is more ethnically and culturally diverse. Millennials want different things than Baby Boomers or Gen Xers wanted. The up-and-coming generation of women *and* men want more balance in their lives. Money is a strong motivator for them, but it's not as frequently *the* motivator. They care about creativity, social causes, and being connected. Millennials want to be treated as partners. Hub-and-spoke management will not work with them. Rather, we have to create a relationship with this generation that will drive their engagement and loyalty. This is an imperative for business success today and in the future. We need as much of this generation, both men and women, in our workforce as we can get; however, we won't be able to accomplish this if we don't change the way we work or the way we lead. Female leaders have a great deal in common with Millennials, including similar motivations and a desire for a different kind of workplace.

Women make eighty percent of all household purchasing decisions, yet the companies who sell them products and services are run mostly by men.

THE TANGIBLE, REAL REASON FOR GENDER BALANCE

My view on gender balance in corporate leadership roles does not come from an academic or social perspective, but from a grounded, experienced executive's point of view: *The reason we need the change has to do with money.*

Each company has the right to use every competitive advantage it can get its hands on, and having gender balance in leadership is one of them. The imbalance dilutes business performance. Gender balance improves it.

> **While the optimal ratio for gender balance still needs research, we know for sure it's not eighty-six to fourteen—the current ratio of male to female executives in corporate America, according to *Business Insider*.**[1]

Many leaders I've talked to don't want to address the issue of gender balance in their organizations head on; they prefer to talk around it in the context of diversity. Although the issue is one of diversity, it's different and must be specifically addressed. The very definition of diverse is "showing a great deal of variety." There is no great variety in gender. There are two, and neither constitutes a minority.

The world is made up of approximately fifty percent men and fifty percent women, making this diversity challenge much easier to solve. Leaders tend to understand the value of ethnic diversity—the benefit of perspectives and thinking that people who have experienced other cultures bring to the table. The different backgrounds bring value. Gender balance represents that same kind of value.

Gender balance in leadership does not have to be fifty-fifty. Balance means having enough of both genders to demonstrate various ways of thinking to the degree that it causes questioning, debate, idea generation, and problem-solving to create healthy business strategies and tactics. What is "enough" balance to accomplish that goal? Is the ratio sixty to forty? Seventy to thirty? That question is still being answered. Countries such as Norway, Spain, the United Kingdom, and the Netherlands are making the swiftest progress toward gender balance on boards and seem to be aiming at creating critical mass.

The critical mass theory—first outlined by Rosabeth Moss Kanter and Drude Dahlerup for the benefit of 1970s corporate cultures—connects numbers with outcomes.[2] The goal is to create enough critical mass of women to change the behaviors of boards and executive teams. They suggest we can do this by attempting to move away from token status, where there may be one or two women, to including enough women to combat the behaviors of a male-dominant group. At the core of this theory is that one person is not a strong enough influence to change the dominant thinking or behaviors of the many. For this reason, Norway, Spain, the United Kingdom, and the Netherlands have developed gender-balance target goals ranging from thirty to forty percent. Though the current emphasis is on getting more women on boards or executive teams, these goals would also work for men, if the representation between men and women were ever reversed.

In his book *Challenging Boardroom Homogeneity*, Aaron A. Dhir writes about the underrepresentation of women on boards and how this lack of diversity may be impacting the decision-making of boards in an unintentionally negative manner.[3] The survey work that Dhir conducted for the book also conveys the sentiments of many female directors through interviews. He found that most women believe their ideas and perspectives are better heard when there are more females present, giving further credibility to the effect of critical mass. Some women, when they're the only female on a board, feel they have to conform to male behaviors for "self-preservation" and to be seen as a productive member of the team whose views are not discounted. Conversely, Dhir was able to identify a number of benefits that boards experience when they have gender balance, including intellectual and experiential diversity. He notes that gender balance leads to a broader basis for decision-making, increased diligence, and better preparation, allowing greater probing and asking more questions—which reduces risk for the board. Most interesting, the simple fact that most of these women (informally classified as *outsiders* because they came from nontraditional networks) did not have prior social circles with their director colleagues reduced the risk for relationships that might influence decisions or support. Finally, Dhir observes that female directors promote collaboration within the boardroom based on their style of engagement—ensuring others are heard before important decisions are made.

It's interesting to observe how we strive for gender balance in our personal lives. Couples who have three boys try once more for a girl, or vice versa; when they have one of each, they're generally content to stop, knowing they'll get the opportunity to raise both genders. And they want that. But in the workplace, we find it uncomfortable to talk about gender balance and why we might want a certain mix of men and women on a team. We find it even more difficult to talk about *how* to do that.

Why are we struggling to address this issue? Do we not understand the repercussions? Do we not believe it? Do we think the facts demonstrating the increased performance of gender-balanced companies are coincidental? All of this talk certainly builds awareness, and that's step number one. So what are we going to do about it?

This is not just an important challenge but also an urgent issue.

For you analytical junkies, consider the central limit theorem in probability theory. It tells us that under certain conditions, the arithmetic mean of a sufficiently large number of independent random observations is the average of the observations normally distributed, creating what's commonly known as a *bell curve*. In a boardroom, or at the senior leadership table, the number of people, or "observations," in the room is typically small; let's assume in this example it is ten. If you accept the premise that men and women think differently (see chapter 4 about brain science for proof), and your senior team has one woman and nine men, the bell curve of observations will be less distributed. And if that group does not proportionately represent your customers and clients, mathematical chances are high that the observations will not lead your business to optimal conclusions, decisions, and actions.

I wrote this book to escalate the urgency of getting more women into leadership so that we can leverage the perspectives of both genders to make more money. What follows in these pages are the arguments for why we need to do something and then some specific actions that male leaders and future female leaders can take to effect change.

As a preview, here are a few big takeaways:

1. You are leaving money on the table and forfeiting your strategic advantage if you don't have women *well* represented on your boards and senior management teams.

2. Hardwiring in the brain is different for men and women. The physical differences are associated with natural tendencies in thinking, communicating, and problem-solving that are all needed in business. Men and women demonstrate these traits in varying degrees. Successful organizations have leaders who exhibit the characteristics of both genders.

3. There is absolutely no reason you should not have gender balance in your senior leadership. It doesn't need to be fifty-fifty for you to start realizing the benefits, but you likely need more women in leadership than you have now. While there aren't studies to verify exactly what percent of female leaders are needed for better financial performance, Credit Suisse reports that companies with women in a third of leadership roles saw average returns

increase to more than twenty-five percent. When leadership is balanced, average returns rise to twenty-eight percent (though based on a much smaller sample size).[4]

4. Defy the norm. Throw out old policies and practices that get in the way of attracting and retaining women. If you want the best talent, you have to compete with organizations that already get it and know how to leverage talent in a continuously connected world. Many companies have already implemented flexible work schedules for parents trying to have a career and raise a family. Baby Boomers who were satisfied with working eighty-hour workweeks and relocating their family frequently for upward moves are being replaced with Gen Xers and Millennials who will trade some amount of money for flexibility and family stability. Companies that will win their efforts are those that provide the work-life integration they demand.

5. I'll be candid. This book is primarily directed at CEOs and business leaders who are, for the most part, male. It's simple math. Men hold the majority of senior leadership positions in all industries. If we can get the men to drive actions from the Ten Steps that will get more women in leadership, the dynamics and performance of their businesses will change and improve. The Ten Steps are the action items that organizations have been missing. Many leaders simply don't know what they should do to drive change. Rather than just describing the need for change,

the Ten Steps will provide the guidance for implementing change. Also, up-and-coming female leaders have action items of their own. Learning about and integrating the Ten Rules for Women will help women develop important leadership skills that will enable them to be more confident and effective leaders whom others will follow, thereby accelerating their own careers. And, yes, men should read those too. It's important that men recognize these behaviors and skills to see how they can support women along the way.

PART I

▲

THE

ARGUMENT

1

MY STORY

I AM CURRENTLY THE EXECUTIVE VICE PRESIDENT AND chief operating officer for The Finish Line, Inc., a national specialty athletic shoe retailer. I'm proud to say that Finish Line *gets it*. When we began our journey of creating a more diverse and flexible workplace, there was no debate within the executive team about changing policies and practices to build our female talent pipeline and retain Millennial talent. In fact, we questioned having any limits on our employees, such as how long a new mother could have a reduced work schedule or their length of time off. We moved to a flexible, unlimited time-off program, giving new dads paid time off to spend with their children as well, and we told mothers they could come back to work on a flexible schedule of their choosing for as long as they wanted. We've kept many talented women we would otherwise have lost and have increased retention and engagement of the young men in our organization. Most importantly, the *why* was communicated from the top. Our chairman and former CEO, Glenn Lyon, took every opportunity to talk to the members of our organization about the importance of making a cultural change in order to get and keep the best talent. It was personal because it was about what was good for the people, which he believed translated to mean it was good for the business.

In the course of my career, however, it's been obvious that many CEOs don't share these sentiments. And, in fact, my own journey to understanding how I could fit into and contribute to the business world was anything but quick and obstacle free. My own experiences and what I learned along the way have helped shape this book.

It all started in first grade. Actually, it was the very first day of first grade—Monday, September 10, 1973. I sat in the front row of my new class in my new uniform and listened intently as Sister Anne Marie introduced herself. She was quite intimidating. She stood tall and erect and wore the traditional habit that most nuns wore back then. As soon as she finished describing her rules and expectations, she moved to a topic that was perfect for first graders: "What do you want to be when you grow up?" As you might expect, some of the boys immediately shouted, "A fireman!" "Batman!" "A football player!" Looking at one another, the girls remained silent, saying nothing because it was impolite to speak before being invited to. Sister asked for a show of hands and said, "Which of you would like to be a nun . . . like me?"

Many hands went up, perhaps out of intimidation or because the girls thought that wearing a habit seemed like fun. Not me. I was the outlier. When Sister asked me why I didn't want to be a nun, I replied, "Because I want to be a doctor or a policeman." Sister glared down at me and said, "Young ladies do not become those things. Maybe you can be a nurse or a teacher." The conversation turned sour when I added, "and because I don't want to wear the ugly shoes that Sisters have to wear." Saying nothing, Sister walked over to me and stood on my feet until I thought my ankles might break. She then said quietly, "I think your shoes are ugly, too." Not another word came out of my mouth that day.

I went home, unable to forget the incident. After dinner, I spent the entire evening in my room coloring my brand-new brown leather shoes with my beautiful permanent green marker. My mother, who was quite unhappy about what I was doing to my shoes, angrily told me I would be wearing them to school the next day, which, of course, was my plan all along. As soon as I walked into the classroom, I could see that Sister noticed them. I asked her if she liked my shoes "this color." She scowled and simply said, "Hmm." That was enough for me to feel like I'd won the debate, which really hadn't started out about the shoes, but about what I could or could not be when I grew up. Little did I know this would just be the beginning of my lifelong conversation about being placed in a gender-based role.

I grew up as part of a large family, one of seven children,

on a farm in rural Indiana. I had five brothers and one sister. Given the number of us, there was a significant age difference between the oldest and youngest. I was third in the pecking order, and as the oldest female, my spot in line came with some responsibility for caring for my younger siblings.

My mother and father had very specific roles. My father took care of everything outside the house, and my mother took care of everything inside. By default, my role largely meant helping my mother. And there were times I was quite unhappy about that. Running a farm meant there were lots of things to do outside, and I demanded to learn some of those tasks, including how to take care of livestock, how to run farm equipment, and how to fix things. When the mower needed to be fixed or my car broke down, I demanded that my father show me how to repair it myself instead of doing it for me. I was quite proud when he'd come back to inspect my work and not have to make any adjustments aside from perhaps further tightening a few bolts.

In addition to farming, my father also worked on and off in the auto industry. It was a tough time economically, and my father had started farming when a long-term layoff from the factory was inevitable. That was the only other thing he knew how to do; he had grown up farming. And although the years he was employed at the factory were more financially stable for the family, it was quite a load for him to run a farm and work long shifts at the same time. That's where the children came in. We all had our share of chores to do every day. And in farming, there is never a day off.

Weather can make this kind of work most unpleasant; it wreaks havoc on a farmer's life. There's too much or not enough rain, unseasonal temperatures, and early or late frosts, and the years of physically challenging work in the elements take their toll on the human body. Breaking up ice in the animals' water tanks when it was two degrees below zero and working in the garden on hot, humid August days convinced me I never wanted to do that for a living. While I have great respect for the farmers of the world, I decided while working on my family's farm that I would develop the means to support farmers rather than be one. I would have a successful career doing something else, something less physically demanding and more financially stable, with some occasional days off.

I admit it. I wanted more creature comforts and luxury. I wanted a house that wasn't cold in the winter and hot in the summer. I wanted a nice car instead the old Volkswagen with a rusted floor that I drove as a teenager. I wanted air conditioning. I wanted nice clothes so I wouldn't be embarrassed wearing my cousins' decade-old hand-me-downs.

Even in my small-town environment, fashion mattered. There was only so much you could do to modify hip-hugging, bell-bottom jeans into something that resembled the Gloria Vanderbilt and Lee jeans all the other girls were wearing. My only prom dress fell into the same category; my mother tried her best to convert a 1970s baby-blue-and-white lace dress into something appropriate for 1985. It was that or nothing.

As unhappy as I was with some of my circumstances, I was not blind to the fact that I had it better than many. There was an Amish community in the area, and their lifestyle took hardship a step further—no automobiles, no phones, and no electricity. As I drove past buggies full of Amish families in my rusty Volkswagen, I was reminded that life could be much different and that many people were happy with far less than I had. I still wanted something different. I wanted the freedom to explore the world and learn new things, and that meant leaving the environment I grew up in.

That day came as soon as I graduated from high school. With no financial resources, I could not immediately attend college after high school. But college was a goal, and I knew I had to figure out how I was going to get there. For the moment, that meant getting a job. I had taken some business classes in high school to learn typing and shorthand, and I was quickly able to line up a job. I was thrilled. I would be moving to the largest town near my small town, which was home to about 35,000 people. That was the big city compared to my rural community of a few hundred. I packed up my car after our graduation open house and moved to my first apartment, with all the linens and dishes my mother could spare.

The professional work world was exciting. My job as a secretary in a law firm came with a nice paycheck and an opportunity to meet people I'd had no exposure to—lawyers, doctors, and owners of all kinds of businesses. I had money to pay my rent, get a nicer car, and still put some away. I also had time to start college classes in the evening. There was only one problem: I *hated* my job. Spending hours and hours behind a word processor, answering calls, and trying to figure out how to navigate the law library was much more daunting than I'd ever imagined. I was terrible at shorthand, so I took notes I couldn't read, which required me to recreate dictated letters from memory. I was typing documents I didn't understand, and the instruction I got from a senior attorney who had a pipe in his mouth at all times was incomprehensible. I began to arrive at work every morning with enough angst to keep me in the restroom for the first thirty minutes and kill my confidence for the rest of the day. I then spent as much time as possible making extra pots of coffee for the office to delay the walk to my desk.

My decision to do something else was hastened by a fall down the short flight of steps from the legal library. I was in such a hurried tizzy to deliver a stack of legal reference books to my boss that I caught my heel on a step and tumbled to the bottom of the stairs. The racket from my stack of heavy books hitting the floor, followed by my landing in a crumpled heap, was enough to bring everyone out of their offices to see what the noise was all about. As my boss (still with a pipe in his mouth) picked me up off the floor and handed me the shoes that had flown off, he said, "Well, dear, you don't have to run." That was it. Decision made. My boss was leaving for vacation in a few weeks, and I would not be there when he returned.

My next job was selling cars. I had an interest in the field and already had some knowledge because my father worked for the auto industry and was always talking about cars. I think he was surprised and proud when I made this career move. One of the law firm's clients was the owner of a dealership. After several conversations, he offered me a job.

At first, I would go to the dealership every evening after my secretarial job to watch instructional tapes and study brochures with specifications on the entire line of Buicks. The owner, Jerry, would quiz me until I got the answers right. Then, he started teaching me how to approach customers. I would sit in the showroom waiting area and observe what all of the other salesmen (yes, all men) did. I listened to them as they answered the phone and placed cold calls to customers. I immediately picked up on how they built a rapport. Of course, being a young female in this business was unusual. I could see the skepticism on the faces of my more mature potential customers as they asked me about a particular model of car. I soon realized I would have to alter my approach in order to be credible and trusted. For me, that turned out to be the secret.

The business was really more about the people than the cars we were selling. It was about getting to know the customers, their circumstances, and what they were interested in. I learned that the biggest part of selling was establishing trust. I also became intrigued by the competitive nature of the business, but what really motivated me was competition with myself. I excelled both at establishing relationships and constantly besting my own accomplishments. This brief part of my career lasted two years and provided a solid launchpad for what was to come.

The next stop in my career was as a customer service representative at Alcoa. While selling cars was fun, it required long hours and working weekends, and it was impinging on my ability to go to school, which I still believed was critical. I actually took a pay cut to have a normal Monday-through-Friday, eight-to-five job, which afforded me the time to attend classes and study. The other bonus of changing careers was a tuition-assistance program, which enabled me to complete my education without the burden of tremendous debt. Simultaneously, I got a *real* education in business. And while I had clearly already received good mentoring, the kind of mentoring I received as a customer service representative was on another level.

Less than a year into my new assignment, I was asked if I might want to move to another town, where the company had acquired a new division. I would have the opportunity to be part of growing a business from the ground up. The prospect was very exciting and very scary. I was young, didn't know anyone at this new division, and didn't know anyone in that town. While I was busy listing all of the reasons I might not be ready to take on this new assignment, one of my bosses asked me to give him all of the reasons I might be successful. That conversation was one of the biggest turning points in my career. Still in my early twenties, I had just received the best advice, not only for my career but also for life in general.

I stayed at that company for almost ten years, and then I moved on to other exciting challenges: a significant stop at a software technology company, where I had some of the most fun of my career, followed by positions in financial services companies, a distribution company, and finally, a large specialty retailer. I've had the benefit of many mentors—too many to name. But I can tell you that most of them, including the two that so positively affected me earliest in my career, were men.

Because I rose through to the management ranks quickly, I've spent the last few decades working with mostly male management teams. At the executive level, they've been almost exclusively men. Looking back, I realize that my behavior was crafted so I'd be an effective member of these mostly male teams. I believe I was not completely comfortable being myself, being authentic, until later in my career. This shift might have had something to do with turning forty. I think something happens to women around that age: You're just not willing to accommodate other people as much as you once did. You stop caring about others' judgments because you realize life is just too damn short to not be yourself. You also realize you are just not as effective when you're not bringing your whole self to work. Not to mention, it's not as much fun.

There were a handful of executive-level women who were also mentors to me, whether they knew it or not. From them, I learned a new way of approaching challenges. These women showed a more caring way of dealing with people, exhibited expert listening skills, and brought a level of rationalism and realism to conversations, which I often observed to be missing in others. They were comfortable in their own skins, not bending to imitate the behaviors of their male counterparts. They also did not shy away from talking about women's issues or interests. They were supportive to subordinate women raising families by providing flexibility when it was needed because they saw the value of keeping that talent. They demanded that the workplace include spaces for women who needed facilities to nurse new babies. They hosted wine and book clubs in their homes, coordinated outings for professional women, and supported conferences and professional development for them. For me, this was the support system I'd never had.

On the flip side, early in my career, I encountered women who were competitive with other women, critical of females who might get in their way, and sometimes downright mean. These women would play extreme politics to get ahead, even if it meant shortchanging someone else's career for their own benefit, or not giving responsibility to someone who might show them up. Their behavior made me ask myself, "How am

I supposed to act? Is that what it's going to take to get ahead?" I believe now that what drove their behavior was the lack of senior-level jobs for women. If you wanted to get one, you had better be willing to compete for it.

Of course, we are all shaped by our experiences. The fact that I grew up with mostly men in my family and have worked largely with men as peers during my career has, without a doubt, influenced the way I interact with people professionally. Successful people learn to communicate with people the way they want to be communicated with. Some of my male mentors wanted me to show more excitement and anger at times, like they did. That's how they communicated with each other. I tried. That style didn't work for me. The successful women I learned from did not communicate that way either.

The most important point I learned, however, is that both styles and both perspectives are needed for a business to succeed. Businesses are complex. Challenges, opportunities, and problems are complex. People are complex, and there are different complexities within the genders. We need to understand and leverage these differences to develop the best ideas, solutions, and actions to have successful organizations. The reasons why and what men—and women—can do about it are the subject of the rest of this book.

2

THE VALUE OF
GENDER-BALANCED
LEADERSHIP

IN TODAY'S ULTRACOMPETITIVE GLOBAL ECONOMY,
even high-performing companies can't afford to rest on their
laurels. Corporate heavyweights spend hundreds of billions
of dollars on research and development each year, fine-tuning
products and nurturing innovations they hope will give them
an edge in the marketplace. Yet most still overlook a far sim-
pler and more affordable investment in human capital that's
been proven to make a difference: getting more women onto
their leadership teams and governing boards.

Companies can and do thrive with men firmly in control,
but given the growing evidence about the business value of
gender-balanced leadership, you have to wonder how much
more successful they could be with this additional resource in

the management ranks. What are firms missing when women are left out of key decisions? What is the real cost of maintaining these men's clubs? Is it worth the price?

FOLLOWING THE NUMBERS

The boardroom gender gap has spurred various initiatives, along with plenty of research to support what is common sense: If a roomful of men can draw on their experiences and insights to help a business succeed, a roomful of men and women drawing from a deeper pool can achieve even more.

In a 2010 study, a group of professors from Carnegie Mellon University and the MIT Center for Collective Intelligence found that a group's gender mix is among the factors affecting shared aptitude: The more women a group has, the better it performs on tasks such as brainstorming, decision-making, and problem-solving. By measuring the ability of groups to perform a wide range of tasks, they determined that it was not the intelligence of group members that affected performance but the correlation to the social sensitivity of the groups, which affected turn taking in conversation, and the proportion of females in the groups. They refer to the measurement of this type of group intelligence as the *c factor*, or *collective intelligence*.[1]

Credit Suisse Research Institute's 2012 Gender Diversity and Corporate Performance report presents findings that show better financial performance and stock market valuations among companies with gender-balanced boards.[2] While researchers caution that they don't yet have enough information to conclusively prove cause and effect, the data is striking:

- ▶ Since 2005, publicly traded companies with more than one woman on their boards have seen stock market returns of a compound 3.7 percent a year higher than those with no female representation.

- ▶ Firms with a higher proportion of women on the board have higher valuations, better returns on equity, and higher payout ratios.

- ▶ In every sector, from telecommunications to utilities, companies with no gender balance on the board have lower-than-average market capitalization; those with three or more female board members exceed the average.

In 2014, Credit Suisse Research Institute expanded research to include data on women in senior management.[3] It paints a similar picture: Firms with women in fifteen percent or more of their top jobs consistently outperform those with under ten percent. And as the leadership team becomes more balanced, results improve, according to Credit Suisse, which surveyed 3,000 companies across forty countries and all major sectors:

- Since 2009, companies with a three-to-one male-female management mix have averaged annualized returns of nearly twenty-three percent.

- Where a third of the managers are women, average returns increased to more than twenty-five percent.

- When the numbers are balanced—a far smaller sample size—annualized returns exceed twenty-eight percent.

Credit Suisse acknowledges that quantitative research alone is not sufficient to determine whether women are making companies better or if the most successful companies simply recognize the advantages of female participation.

"As a former director of a public company,
I know how important it is to have diversity in the
boardroom . . . more than just diversity of professional
experience, industry experience, and education.
I mean real gender and minority diversity,
which brings with it a richness and variety of experiences
and perspectives that benefit companies and shareholders."

—MARY JO WHITE, NOTED SEC CHAIR
AT THE 2014 ANNUAL GLOBAL CONFERENCE
ON WOMEN IN THE BOARDROOM

Still, gender balance on corporate boards has become a point of emphasis among regulators worldwide. Several countries have set mandatory quotas (with incentives and penalties) or voluntary targets with mixed results, though the quota approach seems to be gaining traction faster. For example, as Aaron Dhir notes in *Challenging Boardroom Homogeneity*[4]—

▶ Norway leads all countries, with 40.5 percent female representation on corporate boards; there must be four women and four men on a board that has nine directors.

▶ Spain requires companies reporting financial results to have forty percent representation of both genders on their boards; the country gives what they call a *corporate equality mark* to companies that achieve gender-balance targets, which they can use in promotional materials and commercial activities.

▶ Companies in the Netherlands must disclose the reasons for not achieving gender balance in their annual reports and identify actions they will take going forward to achieve the targets.

In the United States, the Securities and Exchange Commission (SEC) requires public companies to disclose how they approach diversity when identifying nominees for board positions, but gender is not specifically addressed. In December

2009, the SEC voted four to one to approve amendments to its proxy disclosure, including Item 407(c)(2)(vi):

> "Describe the nominating committee's process for identifying and evaluating nominees for director, including nominees recommended by security holders, and any differences in the manner in which the nominating committee evaluates nominees for director based on whether the nominee is recommended by a security holder, and whether, and if so how, the nominating committee (or the board) considers diversity in identifying nominees for director. If the nominating committee (or the board) has a policy with regard to the consideration of diversity in identifying director nominees, describe how this policy is implemented, as well as how the nominating committee (or the board) assesses the effectiveness of its policy."

While the SEC may be attempting to get United States corporate boards to consider diversity when selecting directors, there is no requirement to have a policy in place and no defined objectives or set criteria for what a policy must contain. With such vague accountability, the United States will struggle to move the needle in gender balance as opposed to countries with more defined targets and implementation requirements.

MORE EVIDENCE

Advocates for gender-balanced corporate leadership say having more women in positions of authority would help companies better engage with constituents—internal and external—and develop a more robust pipeline of future female leaders by increasing the number of role models.

Although evidence supporting that assertion tends to be more qualitative than quantitative, it is equally compelling. Dhir's *Challenging Boardroom Homogeneity* discusses how a board's culture and behaviors change in ways that improve their overall effectiveness when more women are part of the entity. These include the following:

- ▶ Enhanced dialogue

- ▶ Better decision-making, including the value of dissent

- ▶ More effective risk mitigation and crisis management, with better balance between risk-welcoming and risk-aversion behavior

- ▶ Higher quality monitoring of and guidance to management

- ▶ More orderly and systematic board work

- ▶ Positive changes in the behavior of men

A 2013 Canadian research study published in the *International Journal of Business Governance and Ethics* concludes that female board members are "significantly better" at making decisions than male counterparts because they—

- ▶ Rely more on complex moral reasoning skills, which involves acknowledging and considering the rights of others in the pursuit of fairness

- ▶ Use a cooperative, consensus-building approach to problem-solving[5]

On the other hand, in this study, male executives scored higher than females in the use of normative reasoning, which suggests men may prefer to makes decisions using rules, regulations, and traditional ways of doing business or getting along. As the study suggests, female directors may be more apt to suggest changes in thought processes that impact decision-making. Change is hard. Could this be one of the reasons why male-dominated boards still exist?

"Having input from board members with different backgrounds typically means more creativity, fresh ideas, and better outcomes," stated United States Secretary of Commerce Penny Pritzker during the 2014 Global Conference on Women in the Boardroom. She speaks from experience: During twenty-seven years in the private sector, Pritzker founded five companies, sat on corporate boards, and helped lead businesses. She said, "Too often, I have entered the boardroom or the corporate dining room and realized that I was the only woman there. That must change—and it must change right away."

Additional balance can also enhance corporate culture and reputation, Pritzker said, given the "positive correlation" to better oversight and governance as well as greater corporate social responsibility. "Diversity in corporate leadership is not solely a women's issue. It is an issue of economic competitiveness. And the presence of more women in the boardroom and in the corporate suite is critical to companies' creativity, performance, and ability to thrive in the twenty-first century."

Consulting firm Deloitte began addressing its gender gap in 1993 with its Initiative for the Retention and Advancement of Women, known internally as *WIN*. At the time, just ninety-seven of the firm's partners, principals, and directors were women, representing a mere seven percent of the total. By 2009, that number exceeded 1,100—twenty-three percent of the management team.

There are organizations that don't need further convincing, such as global personal-care products maker Kimberly-Clark Corporation, which created its Unleash Your Power Initiative in 2009, when only two of the nine corporate officers who reported to the CEO were women, despite the company's predominantly female customer base. By 2013, five of the nine executives were women, and annual revenues and profits had increased.

FUELING THE URGENCY

A McKinsey & Company Women Matter report shows that although seventy-two percent of responding executives agree there's a link between gender balance and business success, just twenty-eight percent see achieving that balance as a top priority.[6]

This disconnect seems critical. Women play an increasingly crucial role in the global economy, controlling more than eighty percent of United States consumer spending, for example, and representing about half of all shareholders.

Developing talent is becoming more important for businesses as old, industrial-age models continue to give way to a knowledge-based economy. Today, more than eighty-five percent of corporate value creation is tied to intangible assets such as people, brand, and intellectual property, assert Cathleen Benko and Molly Anderson in their 2013 book, *The Corporate Lattice: Achieving High Performance in the Changing World of Work*.[7] It's a stark contrast from the days when most value came from hard assets.

> **At the current rate of change, most readers of this book at the time of publication will be dead before gender balance hits fifty percent.**

Change is happening, but way too slowly. Consider this: Sixteen percent of board seats were held by women in 2011, compared to nineteen percent in 2014, when more focus was directed toward this challenge. At this rate, it will take another decade to reach twenty-five percent and more than thirty years to come near fifty percent. The idea that our social values will drive us toward gender balance is not working. What will it take?

TIME TO ACT

Though it's human nature, not bad intentions, to surround ourselves with those most like us, we need to break out of that comfort zone to leverage the competitive advantage of gender balance. The cloning effect that continues to occur by hiring and promoting people who are just like us (whoever we are) is *bad for business*. It creates dominant groups of people who are closed off and get little to no exposure to the thought processes of people who are wired differently or have different perspectives based on their life experiences and cultures.

Is it easy to move away from what is known and comfortable? No. Will it take longer to find people outside of your usual networks? Yes. Will bringing people who think differently into the fold make your life more difficult because they will challenge and ask questions you didn't already think of?

Yes. Will you get to better outcomes both in the short and long term? Yes!

Because men hold most positions of power, men supply the critical mass needed to drive this change. Business leaders must decide now to—

- ▶ Be motivated to take action

- ▶ Recognize the strengths women bring to the table

- ▶ Realize what they're missing by not having balanced thought leadership

- ▶ Hire with balance in mind

- ▶ Take a closer look at female talent around them

- ▶ Develop and promote more women into leadership roles

- ▶ Understand how women in leadership roles will help build a stronger business and a better bottom line

- ▶ Do what's needed to get and keep more women in leadership

3

THE INTERVIEWS:
HIS VIEW, HER VIEW

CONSIDERING THIS CHALLENGE OF HAVING MORE
gender-balanced senior leadership, it is important to know
what other executive leaders think. Do they believe that having it (or not) affects the performance of their business? What
dynamics does having a gender-balanced leadership team create? What challenges do they see in creating one? Is this topic
even on their radar? What do they think is getting in the way
of change?

To answer these questions and examine current perceptions, in 2014 to 2016, I conducted an aggressive interview
process of thirty CEOs and other top executives from retail,
financial services, health care, law, biopharmaceutical, distribution, marketing, publishing, consumer services, technology, and other industries, as well as government. In keeping
with the goal of gender balance, this group was fifty percent

male and fifty percent female. Though I didn't know many of these people and they didn't owe me any favors, I leveraged my network to make introductions; most of the executives immediately agreed.

Leaders believe this topic is important. Busy people in high-ranking positions do not give up their time otherwise. Frankly, I was surprised. I thought they would see this as a controversial topic on the surface and not want to be dragged into something like that. Let's face it, men often talk about how women blame them when things go wrong, and women often do not want to be in the spotlight.

That may be an overstatement, but there is some truth to those perceptions. I intended to find out if men assumed I was coming at the issue from an angle of blame and discover if successful women leaders wanted to be called out as examples. As it turned out, only two executives declined.

One female CEO said she didn't do interviews (a fascinating admission for a public company leader). She did not want to tell her story or talk about how to help other women, though she could have done so anonymously. This gives unfortunate credibility to the belief that some highly successful women still feel no responsibility to help other women. A male CEO said he was simply too busy to take forty-five minutes for a conversation.

Everyone else who I reached out to participated, and I believe most of the interviewees were honest and candid, though it took time and coaxing for some of them to warm up. I explained I wasn't some reporter trying to create a story but a credible executive myself, someone wanting to learn and make a difference for up-and-coming leaders. The conversations were engaging and interesting, if not always comfortable.

I observed that more than eighty percent of the male leaders ended our conversation with an offer to connect me to female executives, rather than additional male executives. Ironically, the female leaders attempted to connect me with male leaders, thinking I might be able to contribute to changes.

Nearly all the interviewees, particularly the men, talked about gender balance under the broad category of diversity. While I appreciate that is how organizations, especially long-standing ones, have approached the topic, we need to remember that there are only two genders among all of the globe's seventy-five-plus ethnic cultures; gender diversity cannot be addressed in the same way as ethnic diversity, which is also important. To bring the appropriate focus to this challenge, we need to have specific, transparent conversations about gender and not shade it under the umbrella of diversity.

> **The good news is that I didn't find any leader who hadn't thought about the effect of having more women in leadership, regardless of career tenure.**

HIS VIEW

At the end of fifteen interviews, I was able to divide the perspectives of these male leaders into two groups—those who *get it* and those who are *thinking about it.*

Male Leaders Who *Get It*

These men clearly identified the advantages of including senior female leaders in their businesses and took deliberate steps to get and keep women engaged at this level, although few of them had achieved numerical balance. "I believed this was important and knew the gender diversity of the team would never change unless I was deliberate about it," commented a CEO who insisted on bringing females into his executive team.

They intuitively understood what women versus men could bring to the business, from the perspectives of customers and product use, as well as leadership effectiveness, and were able to articulate the advantages easily and confidently.

Those who walked into businesses that sold products or services primarily to women, but had no women leading, immediately recognized the opportunity. For example, to them, a beauty division at a major drugstore chain that was run by a man seemed counterintuitive. As one CEO stated, "How am I supposed to best know what products women want to buy if I don't have any women involved in these product purchasing decisions for the business?"

These men also cited leadership skills that women often bring, with collaboration listed most often. The ability to read others' emotions and focus on developing new talent were also on the list.

Many of these men had mothers who shaped their expectations of the value that female leaders would offer as strong role models. As adults, these men clearly understood how to get and keep women on their teams by ensuring flexibility to balance work and family and deliberate gender diversity on their leadership teams by consciously hiring and promoting women.

One male leader drastically changed a very established, large, male-dominated organization's culture by strategically promoting women who would otherwise have been satisfied to stay in supporting roles, much to the surprise of many. He gave them advance notice so they could consult with family and adjust their mind-set to the new role; he understood this step wasn't something he needed to do with men, but he made the extra effort to promote women.

The *get it* leaders recognized that women tend to need or want more flexibility in life than men. This discovery, and the acceptance and the willingness to support that flexibility, provided huge benefits for their businesses. These leaders understood that women are not less productive when they aren't in the office every day from eight to five. Former Radio Shack

CEO and Walgreens president Joe Magnacca leveraged that flexibility. He said, "There needs to be flexibility for everyone, but it is more important to women, primarily due to raising families. In my experience women work at odd hours, but are more productive than men on an hour-by-hour basis. Women don't talk to be talking—they don't want to waste the time." To keep a talented leadership team, Magnacca was flexible himself, often having early morning or late evening calls with staff, instead of conventional face-to-face meetings.

Several men I interviewed noted the challenges that women in their organizations have with exhibiting confidence and stepping up to take on more responsibility. They attributed this mostly to the women's fear of not being ready. Some men were frustrated by this kind of thinking. One CEO gave great advice: "Make your ambition heard. Don't make me guess." He also described the few women in his organization who did succeed in "punching through" to the senior ranks as being more confident, willing to ask for mentoring, and willing to ask for the job.

Men who had female executives on their teams often referred to them as trusted advisors. And they described the women who made it to the top ranks as being in the minority for exhibiting certain behaviors that, in their view, more men did not display consistently:

- ▶ Even-keeled tempers

- ▶ Excellent listening skills

- ▶ Ability to consider many points of view

- ▶ Not making quick, emotional decisions in times of great stress

Male Leaders Who *Think About It*

These men recognized some of the leadership skill differences between men and women but were less articulate about those differences. They were also generally less action oriented in building more gender balance in their senior ranks.

They did voice concern about not having leaders who represented predominantly female customers but offered no new ideas about how to change the situation. Most chalked the imbalance up to nature—that women would choose raising children over their career. One of them said, "It's natural that women choose to stay home to be full-time mothers."

Those who happened to have women on their team described them as having confidence and instinctively knowing how to fit in with mostly male teams in a way that made everyone comfortable, yet enabled them to be respected and heard. Something about these women's style of interaction caused the men to forget about gender, though the women were not acting like the men. This may explain why these men don't always recognize the lack of women on their leadership teams. The women are able to be different but also to blend in.

A former CEO of an apparel retailer put it this way: "Ultimately, leaders hire people they are comfortable with and who they trust. I trusted women's intentions more, therefore I was more comfortable working with them."

Many of these men talked about the women in their lives: educated spouses who abandoned their careers to stay home to raise the children while they (the husbands) worked and traveled. That situation seemed easily understandable and accepted by the men. "Those were different times," one leader said, "and men were not expected to be away from the office to balance the load." Some mentioned the struggle of spouses who tried to maintain careers while raising families and the difficulties of getting back into the workforce after the kids were grown. One executive expressed empathy for his wife, who had earned a law degree from a prestigious law school and had a career prior to having children. "Now that the kids are older, she wants to get back to work. At best, she can only find part-time or volunteer work in her field. She has to start all over, and that's not right. Not only is it not right, it's a waste of great talent."

The men whose wives worked and raised families described their wives as *superwomen*, openly acknowledging that while they tried to provide more support and assistance than they would have for a stay-at-home spouse, most child care still fell to their wife. She was responsible for schools, doctors, care providers, schedules, and most household shopping. All in all, these challenges seemed to be accepted as a way of life, instead of something that could be changed.

> **In nearly all cases of both groups, the wives of these successful CEOs and presidents stayed home to raise children and manage their personal lives. They made a point of mentioning their wives' support and that their careers would likely have been less successful without it.**

These *think about it* men talked about daughters who were embarking on higher education with new career ambitions, and they expressed their hopes for those daughters, which seemed to be different from the aspirations they had for their spouses. As fathers, most appeared to have different expectations for their daughters: They felt their daughters would be able to capitalize on their education and talents. "While I watch my daughter succeed in her college career, I never think about the risk of her abandoning her new career and investment in her education because she doesn't think she'll be able to have both a career and a family."

NO EPIPHANIES

I thought these interviews would result in some epiphanies. Maybe I would uncover something the male leaders thought about that hadn't already been discussed, or maybe a disagreement about the value of gender balance would arise. But after compiling the input of all my interviews with male leaders and boiling it down to trends, I found only this surprise in both groups: When questions about how to change the issue of gender balance were asked, the conversation slowed dramatically.

I got answers like, "Hmm . . . well . . . our company is really focused on developing women. We have monthly lunches and guest speakers for our female leaders. We have support groups for working mothers and forums for the women to share their thoughts and ideas with other female leaders."

Oh, good for you, I thought. "How long have you been doing that?" I asked.

"Well, several years now."

"So what have the results been?"

This question was followed by more long pauses.

At times, I felt like I was trying to sell men on the concept. What surprised me most is that when I put forth the notion that it was men who could change the current gender balance in our leadership, none disagreed. Many silently pondered for a few moments, which only provoked me to talk more about why change was needed and to provide elaboration.

"It's simple math: Men hold most positions of power now; therefore, it is the men who can change the ratio." Again, no one disagreed. But they had no obvious solutions about what to do differently.

> **While the *get it* group was clearly taking more action around the topic of flexibility to keep women in the workforce, only a few were taking more *aggressive* steps, like involing male leaders in the conversation or sponsoring initiatives to support women.**

While there is positive intent around narrowing the gender gap by getting more women in senior leadership, the interviews of the *thinking about it* group reveal a distinct lack of motivation to change it, even among the male leaders who believe it's important.

Talking about change does not count. Action counts. But no one is taking significant action. Some leaders are dipping their toes in the water, doing cursory things that, in reality, may be more for appearances than for effecting change. It's as if they are saying, "See? We tried, but it didn't work. We don't know what else we can do."

These otherwise smart, determined, hardworking, hard-charging, successful male leaders are giving up that easily? Why? They must not truly understand what's at stake.

HER VIEW

I interviewed fifteen highly successful executive women, which included CEOs, COOs, senior partners, and a congresswoman who also previously held private-sector leadership roles. Some of these women hold board seats on public company boards.

> **Kate Quinn, executive vice president and chief strategy and reputation officer for US Bank, discussed the continuing bias about workplace flexibility: "Women still self-select out because of the lack of support for flexibility. It's a bias that exists among male and female leaders. What they don't understand is that they should be using that as a competitive advantage."**

Four common threads were evident among the women who "punched through" and made it to senior-level positions. The first won't surprise you. Of the several female leaders who had children, many had spouses who did not work outside the home as the primary caregiver. They had also constructed strong support systems to provide child care by relatives, friends, or nannies. They realized the impact and value of having this support and what it meant to their success. They knew they wanted careers and chose their partners deliberately, making tough decisions to end early relationships if they felt a potential partner or spouse would not provide the support needed to have a career or a family. In most of these cases, attaining high-level careers was a difficult journey, not because they didn't have the support at home, but because they didn't have support in the workplace.

The second common thread is that they were able to give up much of their guilt and regret about not being all things to all people:

▶ They recognized they were not superwomen.

▶ They accepted that life would not be perfect.

▶ They learned to make guilt-free decisions—without questioning or revisiting those decisions—about when work would take priority and when family would take center stage.

They believed they were setting good examples for their children by showing how anyone can succeed. For daughters, the lesson was obvious; for sons, these women wanted them to grow into men who understood how to support the important females in their lives.

These women also shared a willingness to speak up, step forward, and present their opinions and ideas with confidence. That was the third common thread. They were not intimidated (or at least they wouldn't let it show) and didn't retreat from opportunities to interact with male counterparts, even if those made for uncomfortable moments. Most of the women would tell you this has been a conscious choice—pushing themselves to be seen, to be heard, and to participate—and that it wasn't always easy.

The fourth common thread was that these top female leaders were comfortable in their own skin. They understood that authenticity is a powerful leadership tool and that trying to manage like men or copying any other leader's style is not authentic. Many women cited other female leaders from the 1980s and 1990s as role models for what not to do. They felt that in the past, women could be overly stoic and try too hard to emulate male leadership behaviors. Karen Ferguson, group president of Gannett Publishing, talked about the importance of authenticity as a female leader: "Authenticity enables connection, which is an asset and is more fun. Leaders who create more fun in their teams increase productivity. Women should leverage their natural abilities to connect with people, which motivates and inspires them to do great work."

Mindy Grossman, CEO of HSN, Inc., called the lack-of-female-candidates excuse (as a reason for not having gender balance) a cop-out. She believes that if executive leaders didn't think so narrowly about the skill sets that add value and would do a little more networking with female leaders who could guide them to other female leaders, they would likely get more of the balance they say they want.

The women's interviews held more surprises and differences than the men's. They did not believe that finding high-potential female candidates was an impossible challenge and provided multiple examples of promoting females into senior roles.

The female leaders also more frequently made conscious moves to create solid gender balance in their leadership teams and were committed to spending more time searching for employees if it was needed.

The women cast a wider net and in general took more risks on people who did not have specific prior experience in a particular part of the business or even the industry. They brought these people in because they demonstrated key leadership attributes and had a track record of quickly surrounding themselves with experts who could help them achieve success. In fact, surrounding themselves with leaders who ask good questions was identified as critical. Mindy Grossman, CEO of prominent retailer HSN, demands "a culture of generosity, respectful debate, and leaders who ask good questions, and that culture requires both men and women."

DELIBERATE CHOICES

Indiana Congresswoman Susan Brooks, who described the United States congressional population as "Red, White, and Few," made very conscious choices in staffing her leadership teams throughout her career. Brooks, a trained lawyer appointed by President George W. Bush to serve as United States Attorney from 2001 to 2007, has been no stranger to working in situations dominated by men, as she battled public issues of mortgage fraud, gun violence, drug trafficking, and gangs, to name a few. Brooks brought strong women into her already strong male-dominated teams. Her team was largely composed of trial lawyers, professionals with opinions who didn't shy away from arguing or debate. "While the men and women were equally forceful, I believe we got to better solutions by having that gender diversity of thought."

The female CEOs I interviewed consistently had more gender-balanced teams. They did not as readily accept a lack of female candidates and saw the challenge of balance as critical as hiring people with the right expertise. They seemed to more consistently take a holistic view in determining what the team needed in terms of communication and problem-solving, rather than solely looking at what an individual would bring in expertise.

These strong female leaders also understood their power to attract female talent by setting a good example. "Women want to work for me. I manage work, kids, a husband, and I work from home one day a week," said Karen Ferguson. "I had to get people to change policies and focus on results." Mindy Grossman concurred: "I have a life to manage, and people need to understand that. I tell women to find a path that works for them. As a leader, you have to be committed to making things work for your employees."

Senior leaders who have made deliberate changes to keep female talent have stepped out from the crowd and, in early cases, implemented change that was unpopular. Congresswoman Brooks recalls from her days serving as United States Attorney, "It was controversial to allow young female lawyers who were starting families to work part-time. The caseloads were heavy, and we had to shift work around. We didn't have the luxury of hiring more bodies." In her congressional role, Congresswoman Brooks continues to maintain important flexibility for women who are balancing demanding careers with the needs of family.

When asked how they managed their personal lives, all these women described strong family support systems—spouses, long-term nannies, and relatives. Still, the women who had children took on most parenting responsibilities. The moms were the ones the school called, who made doctor appointments, who shopped for clothing, and who created the detailed schedules to share with spouses and other care providers.

One female leader advised working mothers to understand that everyone will survive if she isn't able to do it all. Ana Dutra, president and CEO of Executives' Club of Chicago, recounted a time early in her career when she was traveling globally for a consulting firm while still attempting to cover parenting duties from abroad. "When the children were babies, I would spend Sundays preparing dozens of bottles so my husband and nanny wouldn't have to make them. I'd come home to realize that I'd prepared way more than was ever needed. The refrigerator would still be full of bottles. And when abroad, I would stay up late into the night helping my daughter who was in a very different time zone. We would fax the homework back and forth, and I would be on the phone with her trying to help her through it. Looking back, I now say, 'What kind of a nut job does all of that? Let it go. It will all be OK.'"

IMPACT OF SOCIAL NORMS

Many of these female leaders highlighted the issue of societal expectations. One recalled being advised by a female colleague to take maternity leave early in her pregnancy, so that male colleagues did not see her in a very pregnant state, lest they have a different perception of her capabilities because they viewed her as a mom. Another female leader declined a promotion because it would have meant becoming her family's majority breadwinner, and her husband (at that time) felt too threatened. It was as if he were failing because that position now belonged to her.

We need new social norms to be competitive in the global economy.

Social norms that have placed primary childrearing roles on women and primary breadwinning roles on men are outdated. To be competitive in the global economy, it's time to eliminate that kind of thinking and establish new norms.

The good news is that the latest generations in the workforce, Gen Xers and Millennials, don't buy into those kinds of social expectations. They want a world that enables the roles of childrearing and breadwinning to be interchangeable, so that parents have the ability to choose and to step in and out of careers and family responsibilities throughout their lives.

4

HARDWIRING:
HIS BRAIN, HER BRAIN

MEN AND WOMEN ARE DIFFERENT. WE THINK DIFFERENTLY, communicate differently, respond differently, and have different natural tendencies and strengths. Women tend to communicate more (women use paragraphs; men use sentences); they are better listeners and are more intuitive. Men tend to be more focused and willing to take risks; they are action driven.

In the earliest human cultures, human beings could quickly identify the physical and social traits that made men and women different. Beyond the laws of sexual identity and reproduction, each had gender-based roles. Men were the hunters and were marched off to war. Women were the gatherers and nurturers of children. While social expectations enforced these divisions, other things going on internally, within our brains, motivated men and women to assume those roles. We were hardwired differently.

During nonworking hours, both men and women talk, vent, and joke about the differences: "My husband can't do more than one thing at a time," one woman complains. "I can't understand why my wife gets so emotional about some things," a man says in bewilderment. We also invest a great deal of time and money to gain better understanding and communication between the sexes. Marriage counseling in the United States is a multi-billion dollar industry for which demand continues to rise.

> **Americans spend an estimated $55 billion on marriage counseling each year in an effort to better understand and communicate with each other.**

In the early 1990s, John Gray published his bestseller *Men Are From Mars, Women Are From Venus*. People flocked to hear him speak about fundamental physiological differences between men and women that cause common relationship issues. Understanding does beget problem-solving, but in the workplace, we don't bother to seek understanding. In fact, we steer away from talking about these differences, pretending that we're all the same, because in the business world, *same* means *equal*. We don't try to build better relationships between the genders or learn how to leverage the strengths of men and women together. It's time to change that. The first step is realizing that we're equal, but we are not the same.

THE SCIENCE

The 1990s was deemed the *Decade of the Brain*, a movement sponsored by the Library of Congress and the National Institute of Mental Health. It prompted, for the first time, deep research on the physiological differences between male and female brains. That was just a couple of decades ago. Until then, with researchers hesitant to conduct brain research on women because of the risk to unknown pregnancies, they assumed there were no significant differences. What heightened their curiosity was the fact that women recover from strokes faster than men and are able to regain more of their verbal abilities.

The part of the brain known as the *limbic system* is a complex set of structures that are responsible for instinct and mood. This system controls basic emotions such as fear, pleasure, and anger and drives physical requirements for sex, hunger, dominance, and caring for others. On a more granular level, the components of the brain include the following:

▶ Anterior cortex

- ▶ Insular cortex

- ▶ Prefrontal cortex

- ▶ Hippocampus

- ▶ Amygdala

- ▶ Cerebellum

- ▶ Corpus callosum

All these areas of the brain vary between men and women and are known to produce different behavioral tendencies. The first four parts of the brain in this list are physically larger in women's brains. The anterior cortex is what controls memories and emotion. While I don't have any scientific facts to back up my hypothesis, I believe this structure is why most women I know cannot forget a mistake they made decades ago, no matter how small, and don't raise their hand for new opportunities as readily as men. Time after time, women I mentor tell me about an experience of not performing and how that memory stuck with them and damaged their confidence. Because women harbor emotional memories of failing, they carefully guard against it, to the point of their own detriment. As Steven Humke, chief managing partner of national law firm Ice Miller, put it, "Men tend not to overthink minor instances or setbacks. Women angst over not getting an assignment. They spend a lot more time trying to understand why they were the wrong choice. Men just move on."

The insular cortex is responsible for perception and intuition—traits that allow women to read others' emotions, a quality many male leaders see as a strength. Time and again, I have observed women in the workplace identify how others are feeling. They care because they understand that if coworkers don't feel positive about the direction things are going, they will not buy into a decision and move forward. In fact, the team will be slowed down if members feel ignored. Women want consensus; men are more willing to just tell people what to do and expect it to be done. As a leader, of course, you have to make decisions and give direction. But executing well requires buy-in. We need intuition in order to determine when we need to stop and take the temperature of a group.

The prefrontal cortex is the judgment center. In women, this trait shows up in the tendency to carefully weigh options and choices while evaluating the big picture, sometimes at a pace that men find slower than they would prefer. I have often observed women in meetings outlining all options when men have already made up their minds and are ready to move on a decision. I have also seen impatience in the men in those cases. There is great value in finding the balance. Yes, as leaders, we need to make a decision and move forward. But it's imperative that the decision be the *right* decision.

University of Cambridge Professor Simon Baron-Cohen's *The Essential Difference* states, "Men's brains are larger and heavier than women's brains. Post mortem examination shows that men's brains contain about 4 billion more neurons in the cortex than women's." However, Baron-Cohen also states that "some (but not all), studies have found that women have a larger posterior section of the corpus callosum," which houses neural connections that enable transfer of information across the two hemispheres of the brain. The question is to what degree these differences enable different ways of thinking, processing, and communicating information between men and women.[1]

The hippocampus controls the expression of emotions. While not all women are outwardly emotional, men and women alike would agree that women tend to tear up more easily when things go wrong. That is usually interpreted as losing control. Even female leaders I know say they can be more direct with men than with women. They don't necessarily see this as a negative but do admit to putting more effort into phrasing their messages to women to avoid triggering an emotional response.

One of the trend statements made by both top male and female leaders was that men appear less emotional than women, and at times this makes men easier to manage. These leaders (whether male or female) found themselves communicating more carefully with women because the women they manage seemed to be doing the same. Cathy Langham, president and CEO of Langham Logistics, explained, "Women get the same point across, but at times are just not as direct as the men." Many leaders preferred the direct communication style of men.

The other three parts of the brain are physically larger in men. The amygdala controls fear, aggression, and action and is why we more often see men take swift steps when there's a problem. Those kinds of responses make them appear fearless, aggressive, and confident, traits that are attractive in a crisis. That is why people are apt to follow those who demonstrate willingness to take risks and take action.

The cerebellum is responsible for motor control. The world has many great female athletes, but male athletes are typically stronger and faster. Though good motor control is not essential to being a good leader, it is linked to activities outside of work that men use to build relationships (such as golf or other sports).

Research is less definitive about the corpus callosum, which connects the left and right sides of the brain and helps us process information. Some studies, but not all, indicate that in women, this bundle of neural fibers tends to be larger and is shaped differently than in men. Other studies indicate that the overall size of this limbic component is larger in men.[2]

In addition to differences in size, another key difference is *how* our brains are connected. A Penn Medicine study led by Ragini Verma studied the neural wiring of men and women.[3] Using diffusion tension imaging (DTI), researchers could trace and highlight the pathways connecting different regions of the brain. In men, they found greater neural connectivity between the front and back and within a hemisphere, suggesting that male brains are well suited for perception and coordinating action. In contrast, females have wiring between the left and right hemispheres that facilitates communication between analysis and intuition.

These variations in the human brain can lead to breakdowns and frustrations in communication between the sexes. *Stay on the subject* is a phrase I've often heard men say to their female coworkers. *You're not looking at the big picture* is a frequent reply.

In *The Essential Difference*, Simon Baron-Cohen describes the *S* brain in males, which refers to a preference for understanding how things work and systematization, and the *E* brain in women, which drives curiosity about feelings and the ability to read emotions. While his groundbreaking and somewhat controversial study was focused on understanding the cause of autism in children, what he discovered were physical differences in male and female brains that affect how the sexes think and feel. One can assume these differences drive preferences in communication, evaluating what's important, and desired outcomes.

THE VALUE OF DIFFERENCES

While every person's thinking and communication style are unique, there are stereotypical gender-specific differences that enable us to see trends in behaviors of men and women. Men love to compete. They love tactics, and they love to win. Think about the predominant male social activities: rounds of golf that call for a bet, fantasy football, or fishing competitions. Exchange of money or a trophy is often involved because that's something tangible you get when you win. Sometimes, the love of winning can cause men to lose sight of the goal. Competition is great, and it's necessary for winning at anything. But for many men, winning means someone else has to lose. When you're considering how to capture market share from your competitors, that's a good thing; when it becomes about competing with another person in your own workplace, not so much.

> **In business, what happens when the room is out of balance? Too much of anything is usually not positive.**

On the other hand, women love to envision. They often fall in love with the *idea* of something, and to achieve it, women will collaborate, commiserate, discuss, download, share, and reminisce. Women love activities that encourage talking: book clubs, wine parties, women's conferences, and children's play dates are examples. They want to help each other and will often contribute when there is no personal gain. All of this social and emotional interaction is good for learning, inspiring, and developing ideas that enable accomplishment of long-term objectives. But just like any other behaviors, they are not positive without other actions, such as competition and tactics.

How does this play out in business meetings? Women tend to shift between the subject of the moment and the broader view, and men tend to focus on the here and now. What kind of thinking you need depends on the situation. Sometimes you have to put out fires; sometimes you need to slow down to make strategic decisions for long-term sustainability and success.

What happens when there are only men at the table? How quickly do problems get solved? Are the solutions long-lasting? Does the meeting turn into a competition over who talks the loudest or who has the last word? Are the perspectives of the other intelligent but less-assertive people really heard or considered? Because men may care more about making a swift decision and moving forward, there is great risk of making a wrong decision when no other perspectives are present. Jim Weber, CEO of Brooks Sports, talks about "red energy," describing the aggressive, potentially less productive problem-solving that takes place when no women are in the room: "The focus tends to be on the what versus the how."

What if there are only women at the table? This also carries the risk of imbalanced conversation and decision-making. Too much time can be spent on envisioning instead of defining and assigning action. Too much energy (and money) may be spent on trying to make something work because of an emotional attachment to the idea, rather than moving on to something more effective. Men will revise a decision more quickly and change course if something isn't going as planned. Women tend to stick to a decision for a longer time. One female leader observed that women behave differently when only women are in the room. The conversation becomes more competitive but in a different way from men. Sometimes information is not freely shared to protect turf. Issues and challenges can become personal because of the deep-rooted ownership and commitment women tend to have to an idea or plan.

BALANCE AFFECTS BEHAVIORS

Balance creates respect. As Angie's List COO Mark Howell put it, "The level of respect in the room goes up when women are present." The converse seems to hold true as well. The female executives I interviewed also believe interactions and communication between team members are more positive and productive when both men and women are present; there's less competing, more listening, more thinking, and more buy-in to plans, solutions, and tactics because everyone walks out feeling that various perspectives were vetted, with every important angle explored.

Here's the reality: *The world needs both kinds of thinking.* At the same time. Especially in business.

When we're making decisions that affect hundreds and thousands of people (add up the numbers of your customers, employees, vendors, and all their families), why wouldn't we want both kinds of thinking in order to come up with our best decisions? It seems dangerous to work without both. Why would we want an incomplete team? We wouldn't send an incomplete product to a customer. We wouldn't come to work half dressed. Most of us don't do anything halfway. So why would we want to consider only half of our best thinking?

5

THE RIGHT LEADERSHIP

MY FIRST QUESTION IN CONVERSATIONS WITH TOP leaders was always the same: "What keeps you up at night?" It turns out, these business leaders worry about three things: finding customers, finding good leaders, and keeping both.

All the interviewees in my study believed in their business model. They believed in their cause and in their product; they saw ample opportunity to find and serve their customers. They were far less confident about their ability to choose the right leadership team.

Time and again, these executives recounted examples of hiring mistakes that resulted in a senior leader not meshing with the culture, not being on board with the vision, or having more self-interest than concern for the company. The few who saw their leadership teams as highly effective described a chemistry between people who trust one another, care about others, and put the company's needs above their own.

Those who didn't have such effective teams were frustrated by not only that fact but also by trying to figure out how to change it. Where were they going wrong in their assessment of people?

I asked them to list characteristics of their best leaders, those who work well as a team. These were the results:

- ▶ Collaborative

- ▶ Good listener

- ▶ Asks thoughtful questions and seeks new information or is curious and innovative

- ▶ Risk taker

- ▶ Sense of urgency or takes action

- ▶ Subject matter expert

- ▶ Not afraid to challenge

- ▶ Participatory

- ▶ Intuitive

- ▶ Wants or seeks feedback

- ▶ Empathetic

- ▶ Respectful

Collaborative was almost always first and foremost; top leaders want a team who can work together to solve problems, not individual experts jockeying for position or competing to win an argument. They want people who will combine all their best skills to come up with and execute the best solution. Because I believe that listening is a critical prerequisite for asking good questions, it warrants being the second most important trait.

A FEW SURPRISES

Subject matter expertise was identified about fifty percent of the time, but with great inconsistency in rank of importance. In some cases, its high position seemed to make sense, such as in the biomedical industry, for example. Yet when I would assume expertise was critical, the executive I was interviewing would deem other skills more valuable. An example is the CEO of a large hospital group who placed less value on having subject matter expertise than on being able and willing to ask good questions of the experts. Surprising to me, in less life-dependent businesses, particularly those leveraging technology or with very long product development cycles, interviewees assigned more value to expertise in subject matter.

In every case, clear priorities of leadership skills and expectations were largely driven by the organization's top leader. If the CEO or division president did not articulate a strong point of view about leadership expectations, there was a hundred percent certainty that a strong leadership culture did not exist, or that it existed in only pockets of the organization where senior leaders instilled their own leadership values. That was a positive, but it made for a culture that was divided and therefore in conflict.

The other surprise was that the word *intelligent* did not make the list. When leaders talked about having smart people, they weren't referring to IQs. As Richard Crystal, former chairman and CEO of national retailer New York & Company, put it, "There are different kinds of smart. Just because you went to Harvard doesn't mean you are smart. Being street-smart counts. [When hiring] I looked for track records, and I didn't hold failures against people. Street-smart people know how to handle adversity, which is always a plus."

THE VALUE OF TEAMS

You've heard it before: A group is smarter than any individual. That makes sense, right? Why else would we have teams? The global business world has long accepted that teams are more productive than individuals. Recently, science has been able to prove that theory, but perhaps for different reasons than we might assume. A 2010 American Association for the Advancement of Science article discussed the impact of "collective intelligence" on team performance.[1] A group of psychologists were able to identify that social sensitivities are the *c* in collective intelligence. When social sensitivity is exercised in groups, the level of taking turns in conversation goes up. Reading others' emotions seems to increase collaboration.

And the level of collective intelligence is higher when females are in the groups. Similarly, researchers from MIT's Center for Collective Intelligence conducted two large-scale tests on small (two- to five-person) groups to study three factors: social perception, unevenness of participation, and the presence of women. These measures combined were identified as *Factor C*, which turned out to be a better predictor of a team's performance than common measures of intelligence (average and highest IQ). And overall, the teams with more women performed better.

When I asked what these top leaders considered the most important characteristics of their best teams, not surprisingly, the list was the same as it was for their best leaders.

While these are the desired traits, many top leaders admitted not having a team that possesses all of them, including the teams evaluated as highly effective. In fact, most did not see several of these attributes demonstrated consistently. When asked which traits from the list their current teams possess, these six surfaced most frequently:

- ▶ Competitive

- ▶ Not afraid to challenge

- ▶ Participatory

- ▶ Risk taker

- ▶ Action oriented with a high sense of urgency

- ▶ Subject matter experts

I suppose you've noticed this is half of the list of desired leadership traits described earlier; the other half seems to be largely missing:

- ▶ Collaborative

- ▶ Good listener

- ▶ Intuitive

- ▶ Empathetic

- ▶ Curious

- ▶ Respectful

So who has these attributes? Why aren't they here? *Because these are the traits women demonstrate more naturally than men.* And if women are not in the room, chances are neither are these characteristics. Yet these traits play a strong role in increasing the collective intelligence of teams.

Top leaders gave countless examples of how women on their teams manifest these skills more often: Langham observed, "Women will more frequently than men take the time to listen and think about what was said before responding." Another leader believed that women's natural ability to be more intuitive and empathetic than men influenced respect in the room. Meeting manners went up, as did collaboration.

Traits that women exhibit more naturally have even been noticed in the medical exam room. Indiana University School of Medicine Professor Richard Frankel, PhD, created POISED, a model for teaching good exam-room manners to physicians, who are now required to use computers to review and generate records while examining a patient. Dr. Frankel observed that female physicians typically look up from the screen approximately every thirty seconds to make eye contact with the patient, signaling engagement. Conversely, the male physicians rarely took their eyes off the screen.

CULTURE FIT

Notice that culture fit—a trait often mentioned in conversations about hiring leaders—did not make the list. Executives do view an individual's ability to fit into the group as critical and see it as a reason why a person doesn't work out. But they don't specifically name culture fit as an attribute that contributes to having an effective team.

> **Behaviors produce your organization's culture. Everyone will try to emulate senior leader behaviors. If senior leaders are untrusting, secretive, unapproachable, and build "silos," that becomes the culture. If they're collaborative, open, and curious, *that* becomes the culture.**

So what does culture fit really mean? Are we trying to hire people who think just like us, who communicate the same way and use the same vocabulary? Yes, we should hire people who align with our performance expectations and values; however, there is a great danger in hiring people who are just like the rest of the team and who will fit in most easily. The danger is lack of diverse thought. Without it, your team can't create the best ideas to choose from, so you won't get the best possible results.

Good culture fit means having people who do the following:

- ▶ Produce the best results, which requires multiple ways of looking at things, then melding the best ideas into the best possible solution, product, or service.

▶ Align with the organization's values. If leadership has established them as honesty, respect, and putting the customer first, then hiring someone who doesn't share those beliefs will not be a culture fit.

A WORD ON TRUST

Another often-mentioned trait of good leaders and teams was trust. It takes time and all of the desired attributes listed previously for people to trust a leadership team. Those characteristics do not have to be demonstrated equally within each individual. People will trust that senior teams with leaders who are strong in a certain trait, such as empathy or risk taking, will help balance others.

A leadership team is held accountable by the organization for decisions they make as a team. This is why it's so critical for a team to possess all of the most important leadership attributes, not just a few, in order to make the best decisions and therefore get the best results. When organizations are performing well, trust increases. Have you ever known a failing organization where there was a high level of trust? Not likely.

*"Aggression is the most common behavior used by
many organizations, a nearly invisible medium
that influences all decisions and actions."*

—MARGARET WHEATLEY

UNDERSCORING THE NEED FOR BALANCE

The world has created a perception that successful organizations should be run by male leaders, because that's all most of us know. Our experience throughout history causes many of us to associate success with traits such as assertiveness, aggressiveness, risk taking, challenging behavior, urgency, and competitiveness. Yet, when things go wrong, what excuses do boards and top governing leaders typically cite? "They didn't communicate. They didn't listen to others. They didn't ask enough questions. They didn't collaborate. They took too many risks." These are the traits more likely to be missing if women aren't involved. Caliper, a human resources firm, published a 2014 study that describes the link between personality and leadership of eighty-five women in senior roles within sixty different companies.[2] As a group, these women scored high in abstract reasoning (which supports problem-solving), empathy, stress tolerance, and energy, which are all helpful traits when leading or interacting with a team.

With more women in senior ranks, organizations will gain the benefits of balanced behaviors and a greater pool of candidates with the skills needed to lead.

6

WHERE ARE THE WOMEN?

WOMEN ARE UNDOUBTEDLY A KEY PART OF THE TALENT pool in the United States: The Census Bureau reported that in 2015, women received approximately half of all bachelor's and advanced degrees.[1] So when young professionals enter the workforce, gender is fairly balanced.

But regardless of industry, when you look at those rising through the ranks, the gender balance in leadership declines. As professionals climb the ladder of their careers, the percentage of women in senior roles dwindles, often reaching teens and single-digit numbers at executive levels. (These studies include Catalyst's *The Bottom Line*,[2] *Credit Suisse Gender 3000*,[3] and Deloitte's *The Gender Dividend*.[4])

This fact impacts the confidence of women who want to attain senior positions. McKinsey & Company's *Women Matter 2013* states that while seventy-nine percent of women and eighty-one percent of men had high ambitions to reach a senior leadership position, the belief they would actually achieve it was only fifty-eight percent for women (a whopping twenty-one percent drop in confidence). [5] For men, the drop was five percent; they had a seventy-six percent confidence level of reaching a senior position.

The McKinsey study also highlighted corporate culture as the biggest driver of confidence levels for women, over perception of capabilities. While many women are confident in their knowledge and skills, if they don't feel they're in an environment supportive to women, they're more likely either to not attain a leadership position or to leave the organization. For example, an organization that doesn't have gender balance, or that penalizes women caring for families by not providing flexible work schedules or maternity leave, negatively affects women's confidence in success.

WHY WOMEN LEAVE

Childrearing is believed to be the number one cause of leaders losing their female talent. This is the assumption employers usually make when a talented female leaves the firm. Sometimes that's what the woman will say; it's hard to argue with that reasoning, and it gets employers off the hook of having a more difficult conversation. In reality, many women leave to do something else they can manage professionally and personally.

I recently conducted a women's leadership workshop and tested the following premise: When women opt out of the workforce, they want to stay home to raise families rather than doing something that enables them to keep and develop professional skills on a schedule that supports both.

Laughter was the response. Most of the women at the workshop said they would go crazy if they stayed home full time, but they wanted enough flexibility to spend quality time with their children and not feel guilty when they couldn't. They knew many women who left their job only because they could not find the flexibility they needed. Those women felt forced into that decision; staying home full time was not their first choice.

Many women in the room were struggling with this kind of decision as well. They weren't necessarily happy with their current job-family balance but also weren't willing to give up their career. One female leader I interviewed, a COO for a national department store retailer, identified the need for women to be able to hit pause during their careers and not be penalized for it. "Managers have control over this," she said. "They shouldn't assume that a woman is checking out just because she needs a more flexible schedule or a little time off for family."

The female leaders at the workshop were also frustrated with having to compete and work harder in male-dominated environments to get promoted, not only to be better subject matter experts but also to be noticed for it. It's hard work to push through the crowd to be able to participate in leadership and be recognized. They said that women simply burn out and decide to do their own thing, which could mean anything from starting their own business to finding an organization with a different environment, often taking smaller paychecks in the transition.

> **Because women tend to value meaning over money, it's much more likely that women will make a career move for the satisfaction of job purpose and being valued, rather than the paycheck.**

Kathy Cabello, president and CEO of Cabello Associates, Inc., made the decision to leave what she considered a great job opportunity to start her own strategic marketing company many years ago. "I worked for a great company, and they did provide me with flexibility," she said. But when the company asked her to relocate, she decided she would strike out on her own. "I had two young daughters and my husband had just started a business. It would have been very difficult to uproot our lives." While she initially worked more hours to get her business up and running and didn't take a salary, the return on that investment was the ability to manage her own schedule and prioritize her family when she needed to, without the guilt or difficulty of managing others' expectations. "When my daughter forgot her flute, or I needed to go to a parent-teacher conference or some other event," she added, "it was much easier to rearrange my own schedule versus one that was made for me."

Jen Petro, owner of DropLeaf Communications, is another example of a talented professional female who decided to start her own business for the sake of flexibility. Flexibility to Petro didn't just mean flexibility with her time but also the flexibility to do the work she enjoyed most. "I had some great jobs and worked with some great people, many who were mentors to me," she noted. "But when you have a job, you don't get to pick and choose what you work on. I wore many hats and had to do it all. Now, I can take the work I enjoy and I'm good at and either decline or delegate work that's not a good fit for me."

Petro is also the mother of three children, and her work-family schedule is better aligned. "After we started our family, I really wanted autonomy and the ability to manage my own schedule," she said. While she has been approached many times over the years to take a job for one of her clients, she's not interested. "I can't imagine ever going back," she added, referring to an environment that won't be able to provide the choices in work and the ability to manage her own time.

Many women who don't have children are also driven to strike out on their own for many of the same reasons. Women particularly want to have personally rewarding careers doing work they are interested in, which often results in the drive to work more not less, but on their own terms.

Nicole Webre, CEO and founder of Livewell Properties, a real estate development company in New Orleans, and also president of Webre Consulting, put her law education and experience in zoning and city planning to use when she started her first company in 2013. "I was unhappy because I did not feel in control of my life and finally realized I had skills and expertise that people would pay for outside of working for an organization." Webre says she works many more hours since owning her own business, but it's because she's energized by her work.

Based on my interviews, I believe more women would like to take the leap to start their own businesses and profit from their skills, in order to have more control over their lives, but the lack of confidence and willingness to take risks gets in their way. Webre confirms this point: "Not having the responsibility of providing for a large family gave me some financial flexibility, but I still had to build the confidence that my business would work and take the financial risk to get started. I withdrew a big chunk of my savings to pay the bills while I worked on getting my business off the ground. Within one day after I officially opened, I had three clients. People were incredibly responsive, and it was not because they were doing me any favors. They needed and wanted my expertise.

I encourage my friends in similar circumstances to take the risk, but the fear of failure keeps them from doing it."

The bottom line is that women leave companies because many companies make it difficult for them to stay. Corporate cultures that are not flexible, pigeonhole people into roles that don't leverage their best skills, and don't recognize or promote women will continue to lose their female talent and perpetuate male-dominated environments. And, as we've noted, based on what all Gen Xers and Millennials want, those same organizations will struggle to keep their best male talent as well.

> **Women are crafting a work-life integration plan that works for them.**

A 2014 Bain study found a sixty percent drop in women's aspiration to compete for top jobs, a change it attributed to cultural challenges.[6] Women don't want to be part of a culture full of middle-aged men telling their war stories and rewarding people for time in the office instead of for results. If women perceive that is what it takes to succeed in a company, they will choose another path.

Women are still taking themselves out of the corporate workforce in droves. The difference between now and the 1950s and 1960s is that they're doing it later. In those years, few women aspired to attain any kind of management position, not because they didn't feel they were capable but because of sex segregation, which was another social boundary that kept men in leadership positions and women in supporting roles. Fewer women completed advanced degrees, and those who did were expected to leave the workforce once they started families. They tended to leave the business world when they were younger.

In 2012, however, the National Center for Education Statistics (NCES) estimated that women earned seven percent more bachelor's degrees and three percent more master's degrees than men.[7] I'm sure these women did not do so with the intention of taking supporting roles. Yet that is where many of their corporate careers end. Women with advanced education are starting careers, achieving some success, and *then* leaving their jobs, just when their value is beginning to peak. Many go on to embark on a different career or start their own business to have more flexibility.

Consider these National Women's Business Council statistics: As of 2012, businesses owned by women made up 36.2 percent of all nonfarm businesses, up from 29.6 percent in 2007, and generated $1.6 trillion in receipts.[8] This trajectory only seems to be increasing. Some may think women are leaving corporations primarily to focus on family, but that is not the case. Instead, they are creating professional scenarios that will make it easier to have a family *and* a career.

Credit Suisse's *Gender 3000* states that the number of women-owned businesses in the United States went up by sixty-eight percent between 1997 and 2014, twice the increase in male-led start-ups.[9] *These women are choosing to work differently, not choosing not to work.*

Another factor that drives women to either leave a company or accept less senior positions is the sheer lack of women in the leadership roles they seek. Women entering an organization filled with men in the top ranks experience big dips in ambition, simply because they perceive it's not possible to get to those levels. My interviews with women who did achieve those positions suggest that many believed they had to make a trade-off between family and executive aspirations at certain points in their career. It took longer to get promoted, because the organization culture (driven largely by the men) made time in the office or on the road a requirement. Conversely, many senior male leaders I interviewed now view this issue differently. Those who are keeping their female talent are more interested in results instead of face time, and they too want more balance in their lives.

We all lose when women leave a company. Businesses lose a pipeline of talent. Women often lose their place in the workforce, along with their investments in education and careers. And we lose some of our best thinkers. This is preventable!

7

WOMEN AND THE TECH INDUSTRY— A SPECIAL CASE

I'M SURE IT'S BECOME OBVIOUS OVER THE LAST FEW chapters that the underrepresentation of women in leadership positions is a serious and widespread problem. So why single out the tech industry? For one thing, the lack of women in technology fields overall is more serious than in other industries. Yet it's precisely in these fields that the needs and opportunities are greatest and where the contributions of women are missing. Reviewing the numbers is painful.

THE FACTS

According to a National Science Foundation 2016 report, in 2013 women were fifty percent of the college-educated workforce. However, women held only twenty-nine percent of occupations within science and engineering (S&E). In the early 1990s, the number of S&E occupations held by women was twenty-three percent.[1] It is easy to see how little progress we've made.

Particularly disturbing is the rapid reduction in bachelor's degrees attained by women in computer science (CS): a whopping ten percentage points between 1993 and 2012. Master's degrees in this field climbed from fourteen to twenty-one percent, but that still represents a far smaller number than those who attain bachelor's degrees.[2]

When it comes to other sciences, women don't have a strong showing either. A report from the L'Oreal Foundation in 2014 analyzed data from fourteen countries and determined that women are three times *less* likely than men to become scientists; just 32 percent of science degrees are attained by woman, dropping to 30 percent for masters and to 25 percent for doctorates.[3]

Yet the private sector benefits from new female college graduates in the lower levels of corporate hierarchy who begin their careers in a scientific field. And the motivation of those young women may be unique. According to *Harvard Business Review*'s Athena Factor survey, nearly ninety percent of women in science love their work. Two-thirds of these women chose their fields because they wanted to contribute to society's well-being.[4] I recently listened to a panel of thirty-three female college-level students present the reasons why they chose a particular field of study, and more than ninety percent of them used phrases such as *give back, take care of,* and *improve lives.* Again, the nurturing trait of females shows up as an influencer in choosing a field.

Professionals who work in S&E fields typically enjoy higher salaries, $81,000 compared to a median salary of $36,000 of the total workforce.[5] Probably because of the labor shortage in these disciplines, these fields also currently provide more stable employment, and because they're better at weathering the effects of economic turndowns, they provide longer careers.

One would think that based on these economics, women would be just as attracted to science, technology, engineering, and math (STEM) fields as men. But for various reasons, they are not. Perhaps more so than other fields, jobs in STEM fields are time intensive and time sensitive. The current culture and environment generally seems to be too unattractive for women to work in these careers long term.

I would be remiss if I didn't specifically call out the computer science industry. Of any STEM business sector, computer science companies as a whole have the worst track record for an absence of women in senior leadership because of a scarcity of female talent in the pipeline. Computer science trails all other industries in having gender balance throughout the ranks of their organizations, with approximately twenty-five percent of computing jobs held by women.[6] Where leadership is concerned, it is a couple of percentage points better,[7] which may help pave the path for younger women to enter and stay in computer science jobs. However, the trend of attracting and retaining female talent has declined over the last couple of decades in the United States. According to "Solving the Equation," a 2015 report produced by the American Association of University Women (AAUW), there were fewer women computing professionals in 2013 than thirty years ago, and roughly the same percentage as in 1960.[8]

What is incredibly ironic about this phenomenon is that technology is on the forefront of everything! All that is new in the world is based on our ability to develop new processes and tools to do things humans cannot. Technology is used to research, to learn, to design, to build, to manufacture, to distribute, to cure, and to communicate, and to do it all faster and faster every day. And guess what? We are largely doing all of this through the perspective of one gender.

Talk about missed opportunity! I'll go back to a few previous points: Women make up fifty percent of the world's population; eighty percent of all household purchasing decisions are made by women. Men and women think differently and solve problems differently. What must we be missing by not having more women in STEM industries?

Perhaps the biggest reason to be concerned about the lack

of women in STEM is that there is simply not a sufficient supply of talent to support the global economy. Countries around the world are already suffering from the shortage, and the United States is at risk of falling behind our global competition. A 2012 report published by the Proceedings of the National Academy of Sciences (PNAS), "Science Faculty's Subtle Gender Biases Favor Male Students," estimates that the United States will have a shortage of more than one million workers to meet workforce demands. The report specifically calls for the training and retention of women, who are clearly missing from the numbers, as a strategy to close the gap.[9]

President Obama seems to be taking this issue very seriously; his administration has launched the Computer Science for All initiative, which is intended to support computer science and computational thinking skills for students in kindergarten through high school. The program calls for $4 billion in funding for states and $100 million directly for school districts to expand K–12 computer science training for teachers, to provide instructional materials, and to build regional partnerships. The National Science Foundation is contributing $135 million to the cause.[10]

Global competitors are also having an impact on the availability of talent in the United States. Rapid growth in Asia has spurred reverse brain-drain strategies for India and China, including generous educational-assistance programs that support education in renowned United States university technology programs and then repatriation for students to work in their home countries. This shrinking talent pool has been compounded after 9/11 by the reduction of H1-B visas that provide foreign nationals the opportunity to work in the United States. Europe is also feeling the pinch. BITKOM, Germany's association for high-tech companies, recently reported that sixty-two percent of its member firms lack specialists in information technology (IT) and communications.[11]

An obvious solution to the problem is to recruit and keep more women in technology fields. If we go back almost eight decades, we find that women were once key resources in this area. In her book *Recoding Gender*, Janet Abbate discusses the participation of women as digital programmers during World War II, running machines that would decode enemy messages. One of the most notable projects was the building of the Colossus, which was an Allied tool to decipher messages—some 13,000—sent by Germany and Japan. Colossus operators were largely women recruited from the Women's Royal Naval Service. These women were known as *Wrens*. Even before the war, Abbate points out, women were referred to as computers, often working mechanical desk calculators, tabulators, and punched-card machines to manage business and government record keeping.[12] But over the decades, there has been slow growth of women in technology fields, and in some specific fields, the numbers have gone backward. What's getting in the way of having more women in technology and, therefore, more candidates for leadership in technology?

UNCONSCIOUS GENDER BIAS

Our society often promotes unconscious gender bias, which is difficult if not impossible to avoid. The physical characteristics of infant girls and boys may provoke different reactions by parents in how they communicate, react, and respond. "Oh, she is beautiful," people will say about a newborn baby girl. "The boys will be after her when she grows up." A hefty baby boy may elicit, "Oh, my, he's going to be a defensive linebacker," followed perhaps by comments about following in his father's footsteps to be a lawyer or a doctor.

Fathers may unknowingly be more gentle and polite with their seemingly "delicate" daughters, than their "tough" sons. They may react differently when a child takes a tumble, coddling a girl versus encouraging a boy to brush himself off and return to what he was doing.

Or consider toys. Toys are designed for two reasons: entertainment and education, and choosing them could be one of the most formative experiences a parent may create for a child. Both game and toy creators have learned to appeal to what they believe are the intrinsic interests of male and female children. Perhaps in the process, we have also unknowingly caused children to form unintended beliefs about their interests and capabilities.

Girls have traditionally received dolls, playhouses, miniature appliances, character dresses (for example, for Ariel from *The Little Mermaid* and Anna from *Frozen*), and electronic games with some feminine appeal. Boys have received what are usually identified as masculine toys, such as erector sets, LEGOs, power figures, race cars, and dump trucks. From the outset, we encourage learning through these gender-identified toys. If our daughters play with what we consider masculine toys, we label them tomboys; when our sons exhibit interest in feminine toys, we call them girlish. The message we send our youngsters is *You should not be interested in that.*

This is even more apparent in electronic games. Video games that focus on shooting, car chases, explosions, and warfare are available in abundance. Whether you are or are not a fan of these kinds of games, they encourage hand-eye coordination and other skills. Where video games are concerned, there are far fewer choices for females, who prefer games that encourage the imagination. The Entertainment Software Association reported in 2015 that forty-four percent of gamers are female, yet almost fifty percent of game genres fall into the shooter or action categories.[13]

Once again, we've missed out on an important opportunity, particularly with our girls, which is to encourage the kind of learning that typically comes with masculine toys that encourage the use of motor skills, versus feminine toys that require more imagination. For example, research suggests that girls have less spatial ability than boys. In a study of infants four to five months old, the males were better at rotating objects than females the same age.[14] There is a possibility that playing with toys that require rotation, such as blocks,

LEGOs, and certain video games, can enhance this spatial ability. Yet these toys are largely marketed to boys, and toys that require less puzzle solving or fitting pieces together, such as dolls, clothing, and play makeup sets, are marketed to girls. We're not promoting the learning patterns that will cultivate ability and interest in our young females.

It may be that toy manufacturers are finally starting to recognize their lost opportunity to market to their female consumers. And LEGO seems to be leading the pack in figuring it out. In 2012, the toy company launched LEGO Friends, which turned out to be one of its most successful ventures. LEGO Friends delivered packaged components in bright and pastel colors to build community venues such as hotels, private jets, salons, supermarkets, and cupcake cafés. They also offer products to build rafting and archery camps. The year it launched, sales of LEGO Friends doubled expectations, and sales to girls tripled that year alone. Since then, LEGO has been rapidly expanding specifically with girls' interests in mind. One important fact they discovered in their research was that not only did girls enjoy the social aspects of building structures that are intended for people to come together, but they are also very interested in detail. They found that while boys more often work on the outside of a finished project, such as putting a fortress around a miniature castle, girls like to work on the inside. You can imagine them adding décor, pretending to play house, or serving guests in their toy-size homes and hotels. LEGO also added social capabilities to their website, so their female consumers can share their works of art with other young female builders.

There is some evidence that educators impose unconscious gender bias on students, something they need to become more aware of. The 2012 Proceedings of the National Academy of Science (PNAS) report cited a randomized double-blind study that required science faculty from research-intensive universities to rate the applications of male and female students for a laboratory manager position. Not only were the male-named candidates rated significantly higher than females with identical qualifications, they were also assigned higher starting salaries and offered more career mentoring. The gender of the faculty member rating the applicants made no difference.[15] For some unknown reason, candidates with female names were viewed as less competent.

LACK OF APPEAL

The slow progress in women joining the workforce in STEM industries may be largely attributed to interest. Women want role models. They want to see that women can excel in an organization. The moment they look around and see that there are few or no other females in corporate departments and in leadership roles, their confidence will begin to erode and so will their interest and commitment. The message they get is that women don't belong. Claus von Zastrow, chief operating officer and director of research for Change the Equation, which is working to collaborate with schools, communities, and states to adopt and implement STEM policies and programs, describes the problem of not having more women and minorities in these fields as a vicious cycle. "Fewer minorities and women in these roles make it less hospitable to those who are left."[16]

One of the very successful technology executives I interviewed, Scott Dorsey, former cofounder, chairman, and CEO of ExactTarget, acknowledges that there's a problem that goes beyond lack of role models to the marketing and positioning of computer science and STEM fields. "One of the major keys to bringing more women into technology is to reach and inspire them during their grade school and high school years," he said. "Many schools either don't offer computer science courses or only tailor them to boys who excel in math and science. Every student in every school should have the opportunity to learn computer science and explore exciting fields like graphic design, mobile app development, website development, product management, software engineering, and much more."

Indeed, the perceived culture, including the work environment, along with the ability to see career growth, has everything to do with either driving out or keeping women in science, engineering, and technology fields, which have the reputation for requiring people to work alone in dark, silent rooms for extended hours. Yet those of us with extensive corporate experience know this is not the whole story.

Technology does not advance without collaboration. Yes, someone still has to write code, but that's the *last* step in the process. New technological approaches to finding solutions depend on collaboration. Scrum teams using Agile development processes to break down complex projects reduce risk and time to market. Up front group brainstorming is critical in designing systems that can communicate with each other in the most efficient ways possible. Projects need project managers who are experts in the business first and technology experts second. All of these roles require leaders who are highly collaborative and who can build relationships and communicate superbly.

I can tell you from personal experience that many of the most successful project managers I've ever worked with have been women. This is not a coincidence. The skills that women more naturally excel at—listening, collaborating, communicating, and organizing—are key skills of a successful project manager. If you are a leader of an organization, you've likely suffered the pain of technology implementations gone wrong because people weren't working together in the right way. When these initiatives fail, it's time-consuming, demoralizing, distracting, customer disruptive, and very expensive.

The way S&E education programs and careers are marketed to females can make a huge difference in developing their interest in pursuing a life path. Take Harvey Mudd

College. In a brief five-year period, Harvey Mudd increased the percentage of female students graduating with computer science degrees from twelve percent to approximately forty percent. For one thing, the school requires all first-year students to take a computer science course as part of their core curriculum. But the college also took three other deliberate courses of action. First, it divided introductory computing courses into two levels and placed students in them based on experience; second, the school provided research opportunities to first-year students; and third, female students were taken to the Grace Hopper Celebration of Women in Computing conference each year.[17]

In 2015, HarveyMuddX was launched, providing free online STEM courses, including computing for beginners. This is a great way for teachers and parents to expose young learners to these topics. What the school has done is neither difficult nor expensive. It just took will and focus to effect change.

ABILITY AND CONFIDENCE

For generations, people have assumed that if there are significantly more men in STEM fields, they must have a greater ability in those areas. Not so. In their book, *Gender Differences in Mathematics*, Ann Gallagher and James Kaufman examine tremendous amounts of data as well as studies focused on understanding the relative performance of male and female students in mathematics. They found that until the age of fifteen, girls outperformed boys on tests that required computational skill. When math concepts and problem-solving were tested, no differences in performance between the genders emerged. However, at around age fifteen, a small to moderate difference in problem-solving favored boys. Boys also performed better at timed tests such as the math SAT.[18]

Lack of confidence may play a role in the lack of women in these fields. Evidently, females don't like being less than perfect, a mind-set that starts at a young age and follows them on their educational path. Harvard economics professor Claudia Goldin made it her mission to find out why only twenty-nine percent of bachelor's degrees in economics are awarded to women. She discovered that if women didn't receive As during introductory economics courses, they were not as likely as men to pursue the subject as their major. Getting Bs in those classes seemed to have no effect on men, however, and men who received Cs were four times as likely as women to pursue an economics major.[19]

In chapter 4, we discussed the connection between the anterior cortex part of the brain in females and emotional memories. When things turn south, women may change direction to avoid potential emotional distress. If women aren't naturally great at something, they are more likely to move on. Women don't view this as giving up but as something not meant to be.

Another factor that affects a young woman's interest and confidence in pursuing STEM fields early in life is the impact that parents, particularly fathers who are currently working in these fields, can have on their daughters, which underscores the idea that men can initially make a greater impact in changing the leadership landscape. In their 2014 book, *Innovating Women*, Vivek Wadhwa and Farai Chideya provide countless stories of women who pursued STEM careers because of the encouragement of fathers and grandfathers who involved them in computing projects and computer games and sent them to science camps. In general, these women had parents who told them they could be anything they wanted to be. I heard similar personal stories from some of the women I interviewed who had technology careers.

Male educators can have a similar helpful effect. Gail Farnsley, executive partner with Gartner and former CIO of Cummins Inc., credits a math teacher for sparking her interest in computer science. "I had a high school math teacher who was blind," she remembered. "I assisted him to read his mail. He convinced the school to create a computer science program, and he encouraged me to take the course. As it turned out, I excelled in this program, which was a surprise to me. I wanted to go to college to further study computer science, but my family didn't have the resources. That math teacher helped me figure it out. He said that if I wanted to go, there would be a way, and he was right." Farnsley earned a degree in computer science and went on to become a programmer, followed by a highly successful career in executive leadership positions and teaching at the university level.

THE SOCIOCULTURAL FACTOR

We cannot underestimate the impact of society and culture. Malaysia's technology industry serves as a good case study. As of 2010, women made up between fifty and sixty percent of Malaysia's computer industry employees, with many holding mid-to-upper-level management positions. The need for technologists, and the cultural connection between these roles and feminism in Malaysia, may have made the difference.

Ulf Mellstrom, a professor of gender and technology and author of *Masculinity, Power and Technology: A Malaysian Ethnography*, has been conducting long-term research on female students in that country. What he discovered is that many Malaysian men do not perceive indoor work as masculine and instead consider it more appropriate for women. Computing and programming are seen as "a woman's world in that respect."[20]

Despite those negative associations, Malaysian culture is advancing education and opportunities for women. In the United States, we have no excuse for not taking action. Women have the access to education. They have the ability. They excel in these fields. We need to build women's interest and confidence in STEM fields, and then we need to keep them in those careers!

WHO GETS IT IN SET FIELDS AND WHAT THEY'RE DOING ABOUT IT

In 2006, a private-sector task force composed of forty-three global companies—including Alcoa, Cisco, Johnson & Johnson, Microsoft, and Pfizer—decided to take action to get and keep more women in science, engineering, and technology (SET) and launched a research project, the Athena Factor, after the Greek goddess of wisdom. The task force examined the career paths of women in SET over an eighteen-month period, producing data that would underpin programs and policies designed to shape corporate cultures and practices to attract, keep, and promote female talent.

The findings won't surprise you. The report notes that women leave SET careers in their mid-to-late thirties, with around ten years of experience for the same reasons that every other industry loses theirs: lack of women in leadership roles, lack of mentoring and sponsorship, lack of support for working parents, unclear career paths, male-dominated departments and projects, macho communication styles, and business missions without regard for philanthropy or giving back.[21]

Notable SET companies of all sizes, however, have stepped outside the box to make some inroads. Examples include Cisco's Executive Talent Insertion Program (ETIP) and Johnson & Johnson's Women's Leadership Initiative. Remarkably, forty-five percent of Johnson & Johnson's 38,000 employees are women, and forty percent are senior managers. In addition, three women hold seats on its thirteen-member board.[22] IBM created a Reconnections Initiative for women who've left their company to assist with education and networking.

Notably, Dupont, led by CEO and chair Ellen Kullman since 2009, has focused on increased gender balance by setting a numerical goal of increasing the size of its female and multicultural workforce by five percent by 2017.[23] She clearly expects measurable results.

The combined effects of more initiatives like these would have a huge global impact. Moreover, according to the Athena Factor report, reducing female attrition by one-quarter would add 220,000 people to the SET labor pool.[24] This issue cannot be ignored. To solve it will take focus, effort, and measurement.

8

THE ROOT CAUSE
OF IMBALANCE

THE ROOT CAUSE OF NOT HAVING MORE GENDER balance in our leadership ranks is *fear*. Women fear taking risks and having so much responsibility that they'll be over-extended. They fear not being completely prepared. They fear being wrong. They fear not playing by all of the rules. These worries lead to fear of rejection and failure, and many just aren't willing to take the next step to find out whether or not they'll be successful.

Men fear changing the rules. This new idea of work-life integration is perceived to be fraught with sticky policy issues and precedents that many leaders do not want to handle. They resist changing long-standing history that defines work and personal life as distinct from one another. They don't want to spend the effort to change their organization's work habits because they can't see the benefit. Those who have gotten over that hurdle can clearly see the payback. Procter & Gamble, which received the prestigious 2015 Catalyst Award for expanding opportunities for women and business globally, believes it has a more diverse and productive workforce since introducing flexible work schedules and initiatives about working remotely. The company encourages and fosters an environment that focuses on results, not time in the office.

There is an unspoken fear by some men of bringing more women onto the team because of social factors. They raise questions like, "How will she fit in? Will she be easily offended by our guy banter? How will we socialize with her? Will she be emotional?"

The responsibility to fit in seems to rest mostly with the women. As I noted earlier, more than one male executive told me that the women on their teams were successful in getting the men around them comfortable with interacting with them. But why should that be *her* responsibility?

There is another fear: the attraction factor, which translates to "We better not hire her; she's too attractive." A few male executives I interviewed remembered a time in their career when they didn't hire the best person (a female) for the job because they feared her attractiveness would bring too much attention to how they interacted. Would others imagine preferential treatment? Would others infer something if the executive traveled or had dinner with the woman, just as he did with his male direct reports? Some flatly stated that their wives would just not accept it. The inferences were harsher if the female hire was single. Yes, this phenomenon still exists! And because of human nature, it likely always will. But that does not make it right, and it doesn't mean we shouldn't try to change that thinking. For a business, the bottom line is at stake.

OVERCOMING FEARS

Here's what men need to stop fearing when it comes to working with women:

- ▶ How she will deal with conflict, candor, or guy banter

- ▶ Emotional reactions

- ▶ How she will react to candid feedback or criticism

- ▶ What others may think if you go to lunch with her or travel with her (if there's a business reason, go ahead; you put the woman at a disadvantage when you don't include her and yourself at a disadvantage by not having her input)

- ▶ How or when she's going to get the work done because she has a family; don't confuse time with productivity

Here's what women need to stop fearing:

▶ Taking risks with their careers

▶ Not being one hundred percent prepared

▶ Being perceived as impolite or selfish by asking for what they want

▶ The inability to have a schedule that works for their life; they can

Here's what *all* executive leaders should be concerned with:

▶ Losing her from your workforce and how you'll keep that from happening

▶ How you'll keep her engaged in your business while she's raising a family

▶ How to challenge her so she can stay motivated, and how you're going to reward her or when you're going to promote her

▶ How your daughters will be treated in their careers and how you can change the landscape for them

▶ What you should be doing to change policies and practices, such as instituting flexible hours and working arrangements or job sharing

▶ How you're going to set an example

▶ Where our future workforce will come from (A 2012
McKinsey study reports an approaching global workforce shortage of forty million highly skilled workers
by 2030[1]; an equal employment rate for women
would almost close the gap.)

If we can make people aware and dissipate their fears, we
can change. A new way of thinking about why gender balance is important and how it can drive businesses—the reasons it's good for everyone—will require additional focus on
women. And that makes some people uncomfortable. In his
book *In Search of Excellence*, Tom Peters talks about our fear
of alienating men if we make an appeal to women and how
we have to stop worrying about that and start worrying about
how we've alienated women to the point where they leave our
companies. And he's been saying that for decades.

Another leader who's worrying about this issue is Gregory
Deason, executive director of Purdue University's Foundry,
an organization that helps turn ideas into successful business models. While attending a conference for entrepreneurial leaders, he learned some startling facts about the
lack of women in senior leadership in the United States. His
response? "Frankly," he said, "it irritated me and made me
mad. We decided we were going to make helping women
entrepreneurs a priority in the Foundry."[2] In 2016, Purdue's
Foundry launched WomenIN, an effort that empowers aspiring women in technology with networking and resources to
support scalable entrepreneurship.

PART II

THE

ACTIONS

9

IT'S UP TO YOU

CEOS, PRESIDENTS, COOS, CFOS, AND ANY OTHER CHIEF anything: The change we're talking about starts with *you*. You have to assimilate this new model, understand the clear advantages, and believe it will be successful. And you have to set the tone for the rest of the organization. Your staff won't say or do anything different unless they hear you say it and see you do it.

Getting and keeping women in business leadership represents such a culture shift that unless you as the top leadership set the tone, you'll never achieve any meaningful change. The organization needs to hear *you* explain why it's good for business and that you expect support. This is an immense opportunity to put your thumbprint on something that will set you apart from the competition immediately and will help you sustain lasting success. It may even be your legacy.

In 2013, seventy-four percent of McKinsey's male survey respondents acknowledged the importance and value of gender balance in leadership, but nearly one-third were unaware of obstacles involving women's ambition, confidence, and corporate culture that prevented them from rising to the top.[1] Once you are aware, you must make a conscious choice to have a gender-balanced leadership team. As a business leader, you are in absolute control of this.

We have very good recent examples of men who have stepped up gender-balance initiatives because they believe it is necessary, including CEOs of Nissan, Kaiser Permanente, Sodexo North America, King Arthur Flour, Cummins, and Duke Energy, among others. These organizations are taking specific steps to change corporate culture and leadership to capitalize on the benefits of both genders. Duke Energy did this by moving a woman into a plant manager role, which was traditionally held by men. Nissan implemented quotas for hiring and succession planning in their Japan operations to ensure hiring and development of women in engineering roles. Sodexo North America's executive committee is now forty-three percent women.[2]

Leaders in these organizations are also leveraging work-life balance strategies to retain more women in top positions. George Chavel, CEO of Sodexo North America, leads by example. He will end a meeting early to fulfill his own personal commitments, such as attending his child's athletic event or personal travel. He was quoted in *Harvard Business*

Review: "Why should women have to be superhuman, have these reputations of 'They can do it all,' and make these major sacrifices, and men don't have those kinds of expectations placed on them?"

> I once had a manager who truly could not figure out how to let a female employee come back to work four days a week after maternity leave. When I asked how he'd managed without her at all for the last ninety days, I could see a lightbulb go off. All of a sudden, doing without her one day a week didn't seem so difficult. You have to help people see solutions.

In the same issue, Ken Powell of United States food processor General Mills talked about his company's raised awareness: "I've had officers at General Mills that say to me, 'I realize that I'm one of several people who could be the brand manager for Cheerios, but I'm the only person who can be the mother to my children.' While some of those women make the decision to leave the company—sometimes permanently—we've learned that we can retain many of them by providing greater flexibility during those hectic childbearing years."

Because men currently hold the majority of executive positions, men are responsible for driving this change. If male leaders don't understand and appreciate the business case, discuss it in the organization, reset expectations, and insist on doing what it takes to build an environment that supports female leaders, we'll be staring at the same scenario ten years from now. Nothing will change. And eventually, because the rest of the world is already ahead of the United States with initiatives to attract and keep female talent, they'll have the strategic advantage to develop into successful global companies that will eat into the United States market share.

When you hear professional women in the United States joking about moving to another country to have children because of a more generous maternity leave, don't think other countries facing skilled labor shortages aren't willing to hire them. Americans have a demonstrated work ethic that many other nations would like to leverage. To compete globally, companies need this kind of engagement. The ones willing to provide flexibility in exchange will get it.

Demand that your leaders develop more gender balance in their talent pipeline. Educate your younger leaders about both genders' strengths, why it is important to have both and why it's okay to talk about it. When they understand that gender balance enhances success, and have tools to support it, you will attract stronger candidates.

> **People won't change what they do unless they understand the why.**

10

TEN STEPS YOU CAN TAKE TO BUILD GENDER-BALANCED LEADERSHIP

THESE TEN ACTIONS ARE YOUR STRATEGIC ROAD MAP to achieving gender-balanced leadership in your organization.

1. **Don't accept that there aren't enough female candidates for your senior leadership roles.**

There may not be as many as you'd like, but they are out there. The business leaders I interviewed who have gender balance within their leadership teams refuse to let it be any other way. They are committed to making the extra effort to fill their leadership roles with the right talent. In their view that includes consideration of gender, because of the impact gender balance has on the overall effectiveness of a team. Conversely, many leaders who do not have gender balance within their leadership teams talked about hiring the best person for the job. While many wish for more female candidates, they do not make the extra effort to find them and did not outwardly talk about gender being a critical factor in the hiring decision.

"I drove gender balance on my leadership team. I would not have accepted anything else."

—GAIL FARNSLEY, EXECUTIVE PARTNER, GARTNER, AND FORMER CIO OF CUMMINS INC.

Having more gender balance on your boards and leadership teams will require broadening your horizons. According to a 2012 Heidrick & Struggles board of directors survey, men tend to attribute the gender imbalance to a problem with the pool of candidates; women are more likely to explain it as a function of established male networks.[1]

That survey goes on to suggest that men and women are held to different standards when it comes to determining who is qualified for a director position. While the number of men holding board seats within the S&P 500 is declining, boards have still been reluctant to hire women who do not have experience as a sitting CEO.

"If I had not been intentional about recruiting and hiring women, I would have been surrounded by all white males."

—STEPHEN GOLDSMITH, DANIEL PAUL PROFESSOR OF THE PRACTICE OF GOVERNMENT AND THE DIRECTOR OF THE INNOVATIONS IN AMERICAN GOVERNMENT PROGRAM AT HARVARD'S KENNEDY SCHOOL OF GOVERNMENT.

Maybe someone with a different industry perspective would give you fresh ideas. Leadership skills are universal. Strong leaders know how to surround themselves with the right expertise, and they know how to ask good questions, often questions that the experts won't ask. Sometimes, the most critical mistakes are avoided because someone asked a question so obvious it sounded stupid.

Smart people can become interested in and learn new subjects. President George W. Bush nominated Randall Tobias, former CEO of pharmaceutical giant Eli Lilly and Company, to be the first United States Global AIDS Coordinator in 2003. Tobias recalls the interview with then Senator Joe Biden: "Senator Biden asked me if I knew anything about AIDS, Africa, or health care. I said, 'No, and that's why I'm the best person for this assignment. I have no preconceived notions about what the right answers are.' The President was looking for someone who had a track record of surrounding himself with the right people to succeed."

Stephen Goldsmith, formerly mayor of Indianapolis and deputy mayor of New York City, made a very intentional effort to change the balance of leadership within his public sector staffs. "The best talent needs to be broad. I increased my chances of having better talent by expanding the pool to women. Those women may have been practicing a different area of law, but they could be trained to be prosecutors. I looked for women who were articulate, could reason well, were present, and could overcome bias. When I observed these skills, I recruited them."

The search for the right candidate will take longer when you consider female candidates. Men in leadership positions currently outnumber women, so naturally they are more readily available. You need to take the time. In this case, you have to slow down to go fast. Put some pressure on your search firms. Don't let them off the hook. Remember, they are financially motivated to fill the role as quickly as possible. You have to give them criteria for bringing you qualified male *and* female candidates.

2. Increase your pipeline of female talent across the organization.

If you want more females in senior leadership, you need to have healthy gender balance earlier in your pipeline, such as in entry-level, mid-level, manager, and director positions, which is where the pipeline seems to narrow. More now means more later. Promoting from within is always a better bet. Where do you recruit? Who gets stretch assignments?

Who is promoted? Keep track of this, so you can push for more gender balance in every area of the business.

Does your current leadership understand why gender balance is important? If not, educate them. You now have the why—the facts and the business case for driving change. Beyond the why, visibility is critical. Call out your current statistics. Make a point of putting it out in the open. People can see gender balance anyway, and acknowledging it shows people you care about this issue. No one should be defensive or embarrassed if your leadership team is out of balance, as long as there is a focus and plan to change it.

Within my own organization, it was fascinating to see the reaction to a simple slide showing the number of men and women in various leadership levels. Many were just not aware of the disparity, or hadn't given it thought, even as we sat in rooms together with many men and few women.

Seek more female applicants for the parts of your business that are operational versus support functions. Credit Suisse's *Gender 3000* tracks—by company, industry, and region—gender balance across the key senior management roles of CEO, CFO, operations, and shared services such as finance and human resources. This research shows that in North America, women in leadership represent just 10.8 percent of operations roles compared to 26.6 percent in shared services. Finance and strategy land in between, at 15.6 percent.[2] Researchers attribute this largely to cultural biases, workplace biases, and structural or policy issues, which can all be changed. There is no reason why women shouldn't be pursuing careers in operational roles; this is another opportunity for men to pull them in.

Women tend to pursue careers in disciplines they perceive to offer more flexibility, such as finance or human resources, and shy away from operational roles that appear to require hard lines around hours spent in the office or traveling. The world is connected 24-7. Your business should not require people to constantly be face-to-face in order to do a job well. Except when creating strategy, planning, or big problem-solving, collaboration and execution should happen around the clock, even when people aren't sitting in the same room together. If it's not, you've got the wrong people.

3. Take more risks on your female employees.

High-potential females often operate under the radar because women would rather get things done than get noticed, and getting noticed has typically been a requirement for promotion. Take a second look around for those who aren't raising a hand but need to be called upon. Do you think that if a woman is not strong enough to come forward, then she's probably not strong enough to lead? Or are you assuming without knowing the reason? There has been much written about the role that female confidence plays in going after larger roles and responsibilities. *The Confidence Code* by Claire Shipman and Katty Kay and *Lean In* by Sheryl Sandberg cite an internal Hewlett-Packard study that reported men would apply for a larger role when they met sixty percent of the qualifications, whereas women would not apply until they met *all* of the qualifications. However, the issue does not seem to be confidence, but rather whether men and women play by the same rules. In an August 2014 *Harvard Business Review* article, "Why Women Don't Apply for Jobs Until They're 100% Qualified," author Tara Sophia Mohr was skeptical enough about the confidence question that she conducted her own research. Surveys of more than a thousand men and women indicated that women more frequently adhered to the written job qualifications and hiring process, whereas men were less likely to do so. Not meeting all of the listed job qualifications and respecting the process stood out as two significant reasons women won't take the first step toward a bigger role, versus their male colleagues.[3]

So the fact remains that men will, more often than women, apply for a job they are not completely qualified for. If women understood the "real rules" of going after bigger roles and promotions, they would likely enter the competition more frequently. She is not right, and he is not wrong. But because women and men view readiness from different perspectives, chances are good that he will almost always step forward before she does.

In addition, a woman may need to be sold on why she's not only qualified but also *needed* in a particular role, why her strengths will help the organization succeed. Women have a strong desire for purpose; the title and the money are not enough. Maybe she's happy with what she is doing because she believes she's adding value and feels satisfaction from the role. None of that means she's not the leader you need. Though men don't have to be sold on bigger opportunities for career advancement, women often do. It all comes down to the reasons for motivation. Hers actually may be more genuine because her primary driver is filling a business need and adding value, with the expectation that the title and paycheck will follow. He, however, may first value the paycheck and be confident there is a business need he will meet that will justify the title and the pay.

4. Create an employment brand that attracts more females and retains the ones you've got.

By default, every company has an employment brand. Whether you have a fancy Web site and use social media to attract candidates or not, what you do have is a reputation. People know what kind of organization you have and what it's like to work for your company, and women in particular care about their employer's reputation. With tools like LinkedIn, Twitter, and Facebook, almost everyone you try to hire is checking out your firm. That is a huge departure from the way job searches used to work. Because social media plays a big role, you need to leverage it.

Proctor & Gamble is a great example of how a company is leveraging its brand to appeal to women. Not only is this approach successful with customers, it also helps them recruit the women they sell to. With campaigns such as Every day is International Women's Day, Thank you, Mom, and The Power of Clean Water, the company is appealing to customers through brands and sustainability initiatives that it knows women care about. These campaigns send a message to women that this company values what women value. Women want to work for companies that share their values.

While not every company is the size of Proctor & Gamble, even start-ups can cost effectively market their brand to candidates. Every business has a website, and most are using social sites to share information and promote their products. Why not spend a little effort to make sure you're leveraging your messaging to attract the candidates you want as well, even if it's indirect?

How can you better connect your business to women? Remember, they have the purchasing decision for eighty percent of all household products and services. Who's leading the parts of your organization directly responsible for product development or service delivery? Who are their customers? If you are selling something to women, you will likely benefit from more female perspective in the business than you currently have. The women you want to recruit take notice of how the company positions itself relative to them and relative to your customers.

People used to ask what it's like to work at a company, and they were satisfied with a few positive answers about pay, benefits, and dress code. That's not the case today. You are competing for talent just as you're competing for customers. Potential hires want to know your principles, what you will deliver, and why it's good for them.

> **A company's employment brand is defined by its reputation. Leadership can define, drive, and leverage it or let it default. A default employment brand won't yield a very good return.**

For whatever reason, many leaders still don't want to accept this new reality. They arrogantly think getting the talent they want is their choice. It's not. You have to use every piece of leverage you can create to win and keep the best employees. What makes a company an attractive place for women to work? What are your organization's values? What is the vision? What do you stand for? How do you support the communities you work and live in? How do you invest in the development of people and opportunities for advancement? Does your culture encourage new ideas and learning and reward performance rather than just showing up? How do you communicate with employees? Do you have a reputation for making sure everyone understands the mission and the state of the business, along with their role in making the company successful?

Last, but critically important, to consider is whether or not your environment lets people work the way they want to work. Do you offer flexible work schedules? Does your business have laptops and video-conferencing capabilities to allow someone to work remotely? How about paid time off for new parents? A Mother's room? Fitness and wellness programs?

The United States ranks *last* in paid maternity leave. Many women here go back to work within two weeks of giving birth. Both rich and poor countries around the globe provide every working mother with paid maternity leave, and many are quite generous, with Sweden topping out at sixteen months. If you wait for the government to decide and enforce what is appropriate, you will continue to lose female talent.

All of these components contribute to your employment brand. If you do not have positive answers to *all* of these questions, you've got work to do. These are no longer "nice to haves;" they are required and expected. These are the things that women and men care about when considering a new professional opportunity. So you can get in the competition for the best talent, or you can let someone else win. If you're doing some great things to build a strong employment brand, you should be marketing the hell out of it to make it a competitive advantage.

5. Keep your female talent.

Once you have acquired these female employees, what are you doing to retain them? Do your practices and programs support women? Budget is no excuse. Many innovations won't cost you a cent: Don't confuse face time with productivity. Create a culture of performance and results. Do you help women work, learn, and develop into your future leaders? Do you consider the real cost of not providing generous family leaves? Do you offer flexible work arrangements? Do you have a work-life integration strategy? Companies committed to getting and keeping the best talent are very focused on their employee's well-being, and that extends to hours not spent working.

Torrence Boone, Google's vice president and head of agency sales and services, describes the company's commitment to "making it an exceptional place" for talent. For people starting families, the company provides extended maternity and paternity leave as well as surrogacy support. It also offers personal financial planning services to help employees build a solid future. While not every company is Google—and some may say the tech firm has the financial resources to fund such programs—they would not likely put programs in place without understanding the return on investment. Your best talent will also demand investment in their development. If they don't feel they have opportunities to learn and grow, they will leave and seek them elsewhere.

Developing leaders is a high priority of successful organizations, and your high-potential talent is looking for development opportunities. Many organizations have blanket leadership programs available to everyone. That's fine if your goal is to communicate standard expectations for all leaders, but for accelerated development of high-potential employees, a one-size-fits-all program is not the answer. Men and women have different development needs, and at very senior levels, it's critical to build leadership skills in a way that's specific to each person. Retaining executive coaches for your best and brightest can accelerate their ability to become highly effective leaders. You will be applauded and rewarded by these individuals for this kind of commitment through loyalty, engagement, and discretionary effort.

A word of caution when matching up external coaches with your senior staff: Make sure you have identified the criteria and requirements for selecting coaches. I could rant about the masses of professionals hanging out shingles who claim to be qualified executive coaches, but I'll keep it brief. I've seen *lots* of money spent on consultants who did not deliver. Agree on processes and stakeholder involvement during the coaching process. Set timelines and deliverables. Hire someone who has—

- ▶ Been an executive and understands the real-life challenges of leading

- ▶ A solid coaching methodology

- ▶ The guts to hold clients accountable

Many women have questions and worries about advancing in their careers that men do not. Keeping women motivated to stay and advance calls for gender-specific conversations about the rules of engagement in the business, which includes speaking up and raising their hands for new opportunities. Some programs need to be designed with women in mind, focused on their specific challenges. I'm not saying men should be excluded . . . quite the contrary. Men benefit from much of the advice as well. Many say it raises their awareness of specific challenges women face in the workforce and how they can help.

But this focus on women is necessary *now*. Once you've created a different culture, where leadership is more balanced, your reputation is solid and your pipeline is full, I believe the need may lessen. But for the time being, this investment in women is required to drive change.

6. Mentor your high-potential females.

Every executive in your company should be a mentor to your high-potential staff. It is a responsibility that comes with being a senior leader and should be expected. Mentoring is typically thought of as some nebulous process where people get together and the mentor gives the mentee, often a more junior professional, career advice. There's some truth to that, but effective mentoring needs to have more structure. Some simple guidelines and ground rules will make it work. How does your organization handle this critical responsibility?

> **Tim Hassinger, president of Dow Agro-Sciences, says the bar has been raised on expecting executives to mentor and develop leaders. "It used to be a bonus that leaders mentored others; now it is a basic expectation."**

Mentors are defined as more experienced leaders who will guide and counsel but not manage performance. Mentors are people who have "been there, done that" and can share advice based on what they have learned. As an example, my former mentors were more experienced executives who shared their experiences and perspectives about complex business issues, such as creating strategy plans or acquiring new businesses. There was a point in my career when I hadn't had those experiences, so being able to get the advice of someone who had was very helpful. I was able to ask questions and identify risks I probably wouldn't have recognized without having those conversations.

A mentor generally should not be a leader's direct supervisor or a formal coach. Mentors are available to have conversations and provide guidance toward development goals along with situational advice. They share examples about relevant experiences. Mentors may also be sponsors, opening doors for future leaders—sponsoring them and advocating for them.

The goal is to accelerate development of consistently high performers who are capable and interested in expanding their skills and roles and have earned the trust of others. These are the people whom others will follow, so you want to grab them and pull them up to the top. Again, don't let the idea of subject matter expertise get in your way. We're talking about developing leaders here, and great leaders are almost *never* subject matter experts. People who care about building up other people are more rare. These people build great teams. When you see someone who has these traits, figure out how to capitalize on that. Observe, critique, provide feedback, empower, encourage, challenge, and reward them with more challenges.

Those being mentored also have specific responsibilities. They should take the lead in setting up meetings and be prepared to explain their goals, experience, and where they need guidance. They should place high value on the opportunity to be mentored and use the time wisely.

Serving as a mentor does not mean you are committed to

a lifelong relationship. You may form a lasting friendship, but that is not required. It's important to share your knowledge and wisdom with many up-and-comers. It's okay for these relationships to be temporary.

Mentoring is a great way to better know your organization. You will learn things about people you'd never get to know otherwise in order to understand their knowledge and inventory of skills. This leads to clearer decisions about opportunities for your mentees to add value to the company.

7. Identify and communicate criteria for successful leadership.

Have you *really* identified what makes a successful leader in your organization? Are your best people the right benchmark? Does every leader in your organization clearly understand the criteria for exceptional performance, not just survival?

You need firm criteria that describe exactly what traits and behaviors are priorities for your firm, which means a leadership performance model as the foundation of everything that influences getting, keeping, and developing your talent. It is crucial that you establish and communicate the characteristics that are priorities for your company. It's important that you create the right leadership vocabulary within your organization. When you identify and reiterate the most important characteristics, you can use those criteria for your most important talent decisions. People need to understand expectations from the start and hear them continuously throughout performance and coaching conversations. This makes it easier to hire, evaluate, promote, and let go.

The traits we discussed in chapter 5—some more frequently exhibited by men (action orientation, risk taking, developing tactics, urgency) and others more frequently exhibited by women (visioning, collaborating, problem-solving, intuition)—are good criteria for creating a leadership performance model to define expectations for your leaders. However, there is no universal perfect list of leadership criteria. What are you trying to accomplish as a business? What leadership behaviors does that require? It's more than just a list of words. Anyone can create a list with words like *coach* and *change agent* and so on, but you have to give those words definition. Those words need descriptions of the behaviors that support them. That's where you need to start.

Create, debate, and come to agreement within your most senior team, then reinforce these leadership expectations every chance you get, until they are repeated throughout the organization and become part of the corporate vocabulary. Use these criteria in every discussion when evaluating talent: in hiring, evaluating performance, and deciding who gets promoted. When that happens, you will be on your way to creating the leadership culture you desire.

8. Establish a succession plan.

Any organization, no matter how large or small, needs a succession plan for leadership, from the CEO's chair to, at least, the director level of management. And gender balance is an essential component of this plan if you want the best thinking. You plan for all kinds of organization needs—having the right ratio of managers to doers, ethnic diversity, growth, transitions, rightsizing, and so on—so why wouldn't you plan for succession? Gender balance should be a key component of this plan. Don't be shy about having the discussion.

Begin by identifying critical positions for the future. These should be your leadership roles. Critical positions are those necessary for leading the functions that run, grow, and transform a business.

Next, identify high-potential leaders. These are consistently top performers who—

▶ Exhibit the leadership criteria you've established

▶ Are willing and capable of growing within or outside their function

▶ Take ownership for their career

▶ Are flexible and want and seek feedback

▶ Earn others' trust and respect

Be certain your top team buys into the critical positions, criteria, and high performers. It's important to agree, because the next discussion will be about the level of investment you make in them for your succession plan, which will require time, effort, and money.

Reaching agreement may be more difficult than you think. My experience is that very senior leaders' opinions vary (sometimes greatly) about what constitutes potential. It's more complicated than simply identifying people who perform; it is not about what they've accomplished in the past but about what they may be capable of accomplishing in the future. One of my favorite teachers, author Marshall Goldsmith, who wrote the best seller *What Got You Here Won't Get You There*, recounts numerous examples of successful people who got stuck in their careers because they were unwilling to continue learning and changing. Their very success caused them to be more closed off to others' ideas. They stopped listening, learning, and evolving.

If your plan is out of balance, go back and rework it. Decide where you have opportunities to develop high-potential females, or hire them to achieve more gender balance. There is no race or time limit on achieving gender balance within leadership, but you should be able to see clear progress into the future.

9. Measure progress.

You must set goals for gender balance in your organization. You need to expect and see movement toward those goals. Be transparent with employees and with your board. Acknowledge your baseline and where you are heading, then drive accountability by measuring your leaders' dedication to your strategy. This should show up in their willingness to engage in discussions on this topic and the actions they take to hire, develop, and promote women.

Change can be simple, but it's not always easy. Keep the metrics in front of you through a talent dashboard, published every quarter for every leader's department. Who's been hired? Who's been promoted? Who has left that you didn't want to leave? Were they male or female? What position were they in? What position and person did they report to? What programs or policies have been revamped? What's still left to do?

Annually, conduct a comprehensive talent review with your senior leadership team. It will probably take eight hours of discussion that will give you a holistic view of your entire talent pipeline and the gender balance of that pipeline. This is the time to ask questions. This is the conversation where accountability is most critical.

Where are high-potential staff members coming from? Where are they not coming from? What are you doing to accelerate their development? What is their next likely assignment? What are the main differences between leaders with high potentials and gender balance in their organizations and those without?

If your senior leaders are not setting the right tone and expectations, your current and future pipeline of gender-balanced talent will disappear. And so will your strategic advantage.

10. Communicate all of the above, clearly and often.

A well-thought-out communication plan that starts at the top is a must. It is your responsibility to set the tone and expectations for behaviors and actions that drive your culture and result in progress. People emulate their leaders' behaviors and support their priorities. In my organization, the CEO writes these communications; my executive team members are active participants in meetings with every level of leadership. We communicate expectations, ask for buy-in, and underscore the need for them to be advocates.

Are there dissenters? Probably. But you would never know it. People who don't agree with an organization's direction usually will leave; sometimes you have to ask them to.

Once you've agreed on what you'll do to achieve more gender balance, make sure those actions are not a secret. From meetings to calls to written materials, there can be no inconsistencies in the message or the expectations. You have to make it okay for people to talk about accomplishing gender balance—what it means, why it's important, why they will benefit, and how they can implement it.

IT'S UP TO YOU, TOO . . . TEN RULES FOR WOMEN WHO WANT TO LEAD

MOST OF THIS BOOK HAS BEEN DIRECTED AT MEN. They hold most of the leadership positions and therefore the power to effect change. Yet I also expect that those who want a seat at the table as top executives will also read this book, both in order to better argue the case for gender balance and to take action to have it. This chapter is therefore directed at women, though it will be helpful for male leaders to understand what their female employees also need to do differently and what they themselves can do—beyond the actions in chapter 10—to help them succeed, in positive ways that make people want to follow them.

These Ten Rules for Women are based on my own experience watching successful male *and* female leaders succeed in senior management roles. I have watched and listened carefully over the years to understand the actions that enabled these people to be called out from the crowd. They weren't all good-looking or even charming. If there was one single common thread it was *confidence*. Successful leaders behaved in ways that caused them to be noticed, heard, and remembered.

Ladies, you need to take the lead here. This is not to say that you should act like a man or that you should not be your authentic self. In fact, you've *got* to be your authentic self. You have to bring yourself to the party. You are unique. Your thoughts are unique. The trick is delivering your uniqueness effectively. If you practice the Ten Rules, you will deliver.

1. Speak First.

Yes, first, not last. It doesn't matter if your idea is not fully baked, with *all* of the possible pitfalls identified. If you wait until everyone else's ideas are heard, while you refine yours or, worse, come up with a reason why yours is not a good idea, one of two things will happen:

▶ You will never be heard, because you'll never get the chance to speak, and the conversation will move on.

▶ You will never be heard because someone else said it first.

Women need to be aware of their own tendency to not speak up. In a study at Harvard College, male students spoke two and a half times longer than their female peers. The instructors were also predominately men. However, the presence of female instructors changed the dynamics of female students, who spoke almost three times longer under instructors of their own sex.[1] If you work in a predominantly male environment, chances are high that a man is leading the conversation.

When you have something to say, speak not only from your brain but from your gut, too. Talk about what you really believe, not what you think people want to hear. Speak *your* truth. If you have a sense of humor, use it. If you don't have one, it's a good idea to get one. Humor is essential for human happiness. It's also an important part of engagement, because it helps people remember you and what you've said.

If you have trouble getting the attention of the room when you need it, there are a few techniques you can try. It starts with body language. Be confident. Don't slump in your seat. Slumping projects a lack of confidence. Sometimes you need to be a little bold. Some of you may think of it as *rude*. Call it what you will. If people talk over you and around you while you're trying to get a word in, try a few different approaches to draw the room to you. Lean forward on the table, stand up, move to the front of the room. Speak quickly and with energy. Turn up the volume. Don't pause except for a quick breath if you need it. If you pause too often or for too long, someone else will take the opening and run you off track.

Let's talk about strategic use of profanity. No one likes a

steady diet of cursing and swearing in the workplace. People who talk this way are eventually ignored. It's disrespectful, and it can derail a good conversation. However, there are moments—and they should be rare—when the occasional use of profanity can get the attention of your audience in a good way. You should avoid words that are extremely offensive, including the *f* word. But words like *damn*, *hell* (as in, *what the hell*), *bull*, *crap* (as in, *that's a pile of crap*), and *holy shit* are generally acceptable to use sparingly in the workplace. Name-calling is a big no-no. And *never* make your comments personal.

Trust me, speaking first takes practice and perseverance. Once people get the message that you demand to be heard and will do what it takes to get heard, you won't have to work so hard to get their attention. They'll be looking to you first, waiting to hear what you have to say.

2. Stop Apologizing.

Stop qualifying your statements. Every time you preface your thought with an apology or a qualifier, you take power away from yourself and give it to the men in the room (because there are likely more men in the room). Stop it! You don't really believe it when you say you're not sure if it's a good idea, right? You're just being polite, because somehow you think the message will be better received if you apologize for it first. Let's think about that for a minute. When was the last time that anyone trying to persuade you to buy anything apologized for their product? "I'm sorry, this car is a piece of shit, but I think you should buy it. Our consulting services might not be the best in class, but we will get the job done good enough." Really?

Do not apologize for anything you've said if someone disagrees with you. Simply acknowledge the comment and thank them for their point of view.

3. Choose a Mentor.

Don't ask for a mentor, pick one. Choose someone who is really good at something you want to be good at. You may have a tendency to try and find a female mentor—one who has "made it." Not so fast. Remember that the majority of senior leadership positions are still held by men. They have the power to change that situation, and there are things you can learn from them. These are smart people who have worked hard to get where they are. You also need professional relationships with them so that you are memorable when there are future opportunities for them to sponsor or promote you.

It's to your advantage to find a male mentor, particularly if you work in a male-dominated business. Going outside the organization to find a female mentor is not a bad idea either, because one may be harder to find internally (again, based on the facts of the numbers). Identify a senior leader in your business who is a good role model and who has the opportunity to observe you. You need to take the initiative here. It's not likely that you'll be turned away. Be respectful of your mentor's time. Have periodic conversations and come prepared with an agenda. Whether your conversation is about how to navigate the organization's political environment or about a business challenge you are facing, be prepared for the discussion by providing a reasonable outline of the challenge.

You should also pick a female role model. This doesn't have to be someone you know personally. Look for a woman you admire, not only for how she can manage a room, but also for the qualities that enable her to do that effectively. What does she stand for? What are her spoken or unspoken values? How does she carry herself? Does she deliver messages with confidence and conviction? Does she really resonate with you when you watch and listen to her? Imagine you are her when you're preparing for a presentation. Role models can help give you confidence. Pick one whose style you can relate to and want to emulate. Practice your style and your delivery.

How do you feel when you see a picture of your role model? *The Journal of Experimental Social Psychology* found that looking at images of a female role model helped presenters give more effective speeches. Participants saw pictures of Bill Clinton, Hilary Clinton, or Angela Merkel hanging on the wall in the back of the room. Female participants who looked at Hilary Clinton's or Angela Merkel's picture spoke longer, and their speeches were rated more highly than those who saw a picture of Bill Clinton. Spend some time watching and listening to your role model. When you hear yourself say, "I wish I could sound like that!" you've found the right one.

4. Make Time for Face-to-Face Communication.

In this ever-connected, 24-7 world, it is easy to do all of your communicating electronically. And why not? Women are such pros at multitasking, so why shouldn't we carry on a couple of conversations at once? I can text with three members of my family while simultaneously carrying on an email conversation with two other people *and* pretending to be engaged in a conference call!

Electronic communication has changed our lives forever, professionally and personally. It can improve productivity but damage relationships. A recent personal example was my husband's request to discuss something we couldn't resolve in email. (Yes, I said it—in email). "Can I talk to you?" he asked. In the midst of texts and emails coming in on my smart phone about some urgent work topic, I replied, "Can you give me just a minute?" (Which really meant at least fifteen minutes). He responded, "Never mind, I'll just text you." Is that what we've all come to with our tendency to multitask? For women who love to multitask—and many of us do—we often miss opportunities to demonstrate our thought leadership and therefore miss opportunities to be seen as a leader, by trying to do too much at once.

Moreover, you can't adequately or even appropriately

demonstrate your interest or passion for a subject or issue that requires debate with your boss, with a peer, with your subordinate, or anyone else for that matter, if you don't show up in person. It's important that women make time for face-to-face communication. Men and women think and communicate differently. Why would we ever assume that we could have an effective conversation about anything even remotely controversial in email? Anyone can make a point better—more clearly, more passionately, and with all of the supporting evidence—in person. And women need to do this especially because it will increase our odds of being heard, gaining buy-in, and winning our opponent over, particularly if our opponent is a man. It's harder to say no in person. It's harder for you to bat the ball back in an email conversation, and there is absolutely no chance of using body language to your advantage if you can't be seen.

It crucial to understand what kind of body language I'm talking about. You cannot sit there with your arms folded. You cannot purse your lips or furrow your brow. Be mindful of your mental state and how it's affecting your body language. Before a difficult conversation, you might say to yourself, "I'm not angry; I'm not irritated because my opponent can't see my point of view." Think about the words and tone that will be appealing. Be relaxed in a sitting or standing position. Lean on something. Stretch your arm out on the table. Use the same body positions you use when you have coffee with friends.

Face-to-face communication is not always convenient, but it's nearly always well worth it. Successful people understand this. They know it's important to build relationships with those who are important to them, because relationships are the most critical element in influencing others and building leadership equity. Leadership equity is the goal: It gives women credibility, and that credibility translates to trust. When we are trusted, we have the confidence to make decisions without always asking for permission. We will take risks and won't be penalized when they don't work out. Women have to be effective at influencing both genders. Our communication style and method has everything to do with that.

So put down the phone or the iPad and walk into someone's office. Schedule a meeting, if you must. If you haven't had a *minimum* of ten face-to-face conversations this week, you're missing an opportunity to build leadership equity.

5. Stay in Control.

Many of us have experienced at least some degree of anger and frustration in the workplace. You may be in the middle of a debate with your boss, a peer, a subordinate, or an angry client or customer when it happens. Someone loses his or her temper. Think about how shocked we are when a display of negative emotion occurs. Men and women react differently. Men raise their voices and swear more commonly when they get angry in the workplace. Women often cry when they are angry. Shouldn't this be OK? Shouldn't we be allowed to show our emotions—whether it's differently than men or the same way? Shouldn't it be OK for women to fire back with a raised voice and some swear words or shed a few tears?

You can do that if you want, but you won't be seen as an effective leader. You will be seen as emotional. While our workplaces are generally more accepting of masculine leadership styles, trying to act like the men won't work for women because we will be seen as disingenuous. If we cry, we are seen as weak. Of course, if men cry, they may be seen as caring and genuine; remember former Speaker of the House John Boehner? Boehner demonstrated his inability to hold back tears from such deserving events as Pope Francis's visiting speech in Washington, DC in 2015, an interview about opportunities for kids on the Golf Channel, and his own commencement address to graduates of Ohio State University in 2011. There is a double standard when it comes to displaying emotion in the workplace.

Conversely, don't be quick to act the peacemaker. Women have a natural reflex to smooth a situation over and make a conflict go way. It's not your job to make a disagreement disappear. This is the time to push outside your comfort zone. Don't apologize (unless you were the one who made the outburst). Don't offer up a solution just to appease others. Don't get upset. And don't lose track of the issue at hand. Ignore the outburst. Count to five if you need to buy a bit of time. It's OK to have uncomfortable silence. If you want to diffuse an issue, ask questions. Stay engaged, stay focused, and *don't* become defensive. Continue the conversation to keep the discussion on track. If there's no way to keep going, then suggest a break and schedule a time to reconvene. Resist the tendency to avoid returning to the discussion. That's the easy thing to do. Push past that fear and get back to it.

This is a particularly difficult skill to master, but it is a skill, and you can practice it. To do this, you first must take the emotion out of the conversation. What is your goal? What is the other person's goal? Start there. Have a conversation about that. Don't assume either of you know what the other's goal is. When you take a step back and start from the beginning, you almost always land in a good place, which will be the foundation for creating next steps.

If you can predict or are planning on having a difficult conversation, it's important to prepare. What words will you choose? Can you anticipate the response? Can you influence the timing? Practicing in your head is a good way to begin. You can also ask a close friend or spouse to role-play with you. Have them ask you the questions and make the comments you know will push your buttons. Practice your responses. You'll know you've got the hang of it when someone says something that just created a twinge of irritation, but you responded appropriately and stayed in control. As Margaret Thatcher once said, "To wear your heart on your sleeve isn't a very good plan; you should wear it on the inside where it functions best."

6. Give Up the Guilt.

The demands on everyone's time in a continuously connected world have never been greater. And for many professional women, there are often added responsibilities connected to taking care of other people. Our attempts to do everything for everyone flow out of a natural instinct to nurture, which is then fueled by guilt. Guilt causes women to overcommit, take care of others first, and put their own needs at the very back of the line.

As I mentioned earlier, however, women who have reached top leadership roles have learned how to push guilt to the side. That's not to say that these women didn't sometimes feel guilty or perhaps inadequate while trying to balance work and family. One successful female executive recalled a time when her five-year-old daughter called her out on some behavior obviously provoked by guilt. On a Sunday afternoon, her daughter asked her if she was going on a trip the next day. Her mother replied honestly and said, "Yes, I am, honey. I was going to tell you later." Her daughter replied, "I thought so, because you're being extra nice to me today."

The United States Bureau of Labor Statistics published a survey that says men are more likely to participate in sports, exercise, or recreation on any given day. And when they do participate, they do it for longer periods of time than women. They will take the time to refuel themselves on a more consistent basis. Right or wrong, the truth is men are better about taking care of themselves in that way than women.

One CEO of a large hospital network talked about the physical well-being of the network's nurses. Nurses, who are mostly women, are so focused on taking care of others that they forget or don't take time to take care of themselves. And they work in health care. Remember the rule about oxygen masks on planes? They always tell you to put your own on first and then help others. The same thing applies to women in business. We have to realize we often give too much of ourselves.

Another way to eliminate guilt is to be selfish with your time. Women have a more difficult time than men saying no to requests that they really don't want to do, whether for work, personal life, or the community. Prioritize your time. Spend it doing what is important to you and what you care about. Invest your time in what you *want* to do, what gives you the most satisfaction, and what provides the most value. If a request doesn't fall into that category, be prepared with a polite no: "I would love to participate, but my plate is full right now. I just won't be able to make that commitment."

If having a career and a family is important to you, then have it. There will be times when one or the other will come first. When you make that decision, don't revisit it. Shut out the doubt.

Guilt is a very strong source of motivation. It keeps us

moving from one task to the next, until we are ready to spin out of control or collapse. Guilt provokes us to create new standards for multitasking. Simultaneously conducting a conference call, reading our email, eating our lunch, and online shopping for our niece's wedding gift is all too common. Stop it! Be present. Be focused. Be aware. You don't have to do everything all at the same time. No one expects that except you. And if they do, reset their expectations. You will be much happier, and others will be pleased to be around you, because they will have more of your undistracted attention. You will reduce your stress level as well, which might help you live longer because you will have *more time to do more rather than more to do in less time.*

7. Ask for What You Want.

Take a look around at the successful men in your organization. How many examples do you see of men who have succeeded because they raised their hand for an opportunity? Perhaps you don't think they should have gotten it. Maybe you think they should have been turned down. Well, that doesn't matter. They are there.

As a senior female executive, I've seen it a million times. Over and over again, men in my organizations have stepped forward for a role they were not ready for. More than half of the time they landed the job simply because they asked. Were they being selfish? Sure. Is that wrong? Think carefully before you answer that.

The truth is women need to be selfish when it comes to opportunities. You don't have to wait until something is offered to you in order to obtain it. You should be thinking about what you want to do next and making sure that people in control of those decisions are aware of your aims. Remind them frequently. Ask for the opportunity well before you think you are ready. If you don't, someone else will, and chances are good that they're not ready either.

Be selfish when it comes to money as well. We all know the statistics: Women make seventy to eighty cents for every dollar a man earns, depending on whose data you use. The point is it's a big difference. But women must take some responsibility for this, too. Women don't make less money than men because men decided that women should be paid less. That may have held true several decades ago, when the excuse was that men had families to support. Now, however, I believe this situation has sustained itself because men ask and women don't. Ask for the money you deserve and don't question whether you deserve it or not. Procrastination will cost you. The long-term effect on your bank account is a six-figure number.

On this point, it is important that you are your own agent. Don't go to human resources. Don't ask someone else to make the case on your behalf because you don't have the courage or you don't want to put your boss on the spot. I can tell you from personal experience that it won't work. When you make the case yourself, you will make a better case, and, more importantly, it's a lot harder for your supervisor to say no to *you* than it is to turn down your representative.

8. Play to Win.

Don't be afraid to press your point, to press it hard, and to keep pressing. Women are afraid to takes risks in ways that men are not. But we need to be more resilient. Take a look around at the people you know who are successful—both women and men. Are their feelings hurt or are they emotionally scarred when someone disagrees with them? Do they stop speaking up? Do they ask permission before taking any action? The answer is no. You need to get comfortable with the idea of rejection in pursuit of your aim.

During a time of frustration in my career, I was told by one of my mentors, "It's just a game. Play the game, and play to win." Why does it seem that we have to work harder to convince others (usually men) that our idea, approach, or plan is the best one? Can't they see the logic in it? Women often hate being persistent. They don't think they should have to present an idea or opinion more than once for it to be heard. This is because women, in general, find this behavior annoying. "I heard you the first time" is usually the response you will get from a woman to whom you repeat a request. But for men, the perception is different. They often need to hear an idea more than once to digest it. The first reaction is usually opposition to the idea, based on some experience or preconceived notion. The second reaction is to listen a little more closely and digest it. The third reaction is to make it their own. I once told one of my former male executive colleagues, "I know I always have to present an idea to you three times before I have a chance of getting your agreement." And when he thought about that, he absolutely agreed. Yes, it can be exhausting. But you have a choice. Either play to win or just sit on the sidelines and be frustrated.

What do you have to lose by not fighting for what you want, by not speaking up, not stepping forward, not asking for money, or not making a decision, and by not ever failing? The answer is *everything*. You will lose the opportunity to be heard, to be valued, to make a bigger impact, and probably the chance to make more money, if that's important to you. What you have to gain, in addition to all of those things, is increased self-confidence and satisfaction from the life you're living.

I don't know about you, but personally, I don't want to go along to get along. It's much more fun to work hard and argue hard for a good reason—even if I lose that particular argument—than it is to shut up and take the easy road. "Isn't that risky?" you may ask. It can be. There's good reason to pick your battles. There are good reasons to sometimes let someone else win. You have to weigh the value of your idea or goal. Is it important enough to you to spend the extra energy to influence others? Why? Does it impact other people? How? Will you sleep better knowing you tried, whether you're successful or not? If you care, then you need to play the game to win.

Playing to win means you have to invest in relationships. (See number 4 about face-to-face communication.) Do you think that when a group of guys in your department goes to lunch together or with the boss that the discussion is only about sports and their kids? When you see men sitting in each other's offices chatting with their legs crossed, with no notebook or pen in sight, that they are just shooting the breeze about last night's big game? Sure, sometimes they are. But plenty of time is also spent on attempts to influence one another's thinking about something business related. Everyone has an agenda. You should have an agenda, too. And instead of retreating, you should invest the time in social conversation that helps build those relationships. Go to lunch with colleagues, both men and women. Take advantage of casual conversations, meals, or business trips with those you work with and work for. Make a point of social interaction with colleagues you don't know well. It will help you build trusting relationships that will enable you to get things done in the workplace.

I feel as if I always win, obviously not with every issue at hand, but I always win the opportunity to shape others' thinking. When I've made the extra effort and taken the risk to influence others for a good reason, I believe I've made an impact on how people will think about some future question. I hope our interaction will affect the way they make future decisions, too. All of that means taking risks. You have to have courage. Don't be afraid to debate. Don't be afraid to be told no. Have the courage and resilience to play the game to win.

9. Make Deposits in the Emotional Bank.

Making deposits in the emotional bank is the area where leaders of both genders can improve the most. As leaders, we are generally focused on what is wrong, on what needs to be fixed. That's natural, because by default, we need to be improving something that is important and broken in order to feel we're adding value. But with this habit comes the unintended consequence of not taking the time out to celebrate wins and appreciate people. Recognizing others for good work is an opportunity that women can leverage, because women have a natural tendency to do this more often. They generally get higher ratings for providing more frequent feedback than male managers. But none of us, male or female, do it nearly enough.

Recall how you felt the last time you did something you thought was really great work and no one said a word. Maybe you didn't mind, because, after all, great work is the standard expectation and you expect it from yourself, too. You're paid well, so you think that's recognition enough. But think about how you felt when someone made the effort to tell you about something you could have done better. While you smiled and thanked them for the feedback, I'm willing to bet that the little voice in your head was saying something else. And it likely wasn't good.

You've probably heard it said that people leave managers, not organizations. Lack of acknowledgment of good work is a big part of that equation. Recognize someone's good performance in the moment if you can. If you didn't do it in the moment, do it now. It's never too late. Each time you respond in this way, you make a deposit in someone's emotional bank. As a leader, you need a solid balance in this bank, because there will be times when you need to make a withdrawal and give tough feedback. If your balance is negative, you have no credit to draw against. This is where women should leverage their natural inclination to nurture. Making emotional deposits with peers, subordinates, and even your boss will make you a stronger leader and a great role model.

There are going to be times when the people you are bringing up behind you are going to disappoint you. After all, they have a lot to learn in this world. It is your job as their leader to guide them and protect them within reason (without overprotecting them). Once in a while, they are going to step off the path. In an effort to make a name for themselves, they will do something without your approval that will create a mess that you must clean up or that hurts you or your reputation. Help people learn from their mistakes. Coach them. You will be teaching someone else a very important lesson in life—a lesson of loyalty, belief, commitment, and the value of a second chance.

10. Keep Your Company's Female Talent.

Women have a vested interest in changing the ratio of female leaders in our country, whether it is in business or in government. And for women in leadership roles, they need to do their part. There is power in numbers, and the effect of having role models in numbers can't be overestimated. *Huffington Post Women* published the results of research done on the West Bengal of India. In that region, there have been quotas in place for female politicians since 1993. The research found that in areas with long-serving female leaders, the gender gap in teen education goals disappeared. Parents and teens alike began setting more ambitious education goals for themselves and their daughters.[2] Seeing women in charge changes perceptions by women and men alike. Ambitions and expectations change.

If you are in a position of power, you have a unique opportunity to help other women. Sallie Krawcheck, one of the top women on Wall Street and former head of wealth management at both Citigroup and Merrill Lynch, is putting her name and influence behind an investment vehicle that will direct assets to companies who put women in leadership positions.

Christine LaGarde, managing director of the International Monetary Fund, is the first woman to run the 188-country financial organization and is a well-known advocate for women in the workforce. Says LaGarde, "I know this is economic jargon, but essentially, if you bring more women to the job market, you create value, it makes economic sense, and growth is improved. There are countries where it's almost a no-brainer: Korea, Japan, soon to be China, certainly Germany, Italy. Why? Because they have an aging population."

Women often work behind the scenes. Because we naturally focus on what needs to be done, rather than being noticed, women often do not get the recognition they deserve. If you are in a position of power, it means people are already listening to you. Use that power to recognize the good work of other women, in front of everyone, especially men. When they realize how these talented women can help them achieve their goals, they will be motivated to recruit and promote them. And so the movement toward the creation of critical mass begins.

Let's also use our power to keep up-and-coming female leaders in the workforce. I see many women opt out of the workplace at the point in their lives when they start families. I understand that it's hard to have the time and energy to do it all. But when they leave the business world, we all lose. We lose the thought leadership of these smart, talented women and our companies are the worse for that.

These women who opt out of the workforce also lose, if not now, then later in life. How many times have you seen it? A friend or acquaintance who left the business world to raise a family ten, fifteen, or twenty years ago is now at a crossroads and doesn't know what to do. Perhaps the kids have gone off to college or the marriage is at an end. The woman either wants or needs to rejoin the workforce. But it's impossible for her to return to where she left off. In fact, she may not get back into her field at all. She is left without power and without a choice she wants.

All leaders in positions of power can change this. You should want to change this and feel a responsibility to do so. It is not easy. You have to influence your organization to change its policies, practices, and culture to create flexible schedules, job sharing, and other opportunities to support working parents. Help create a workplace that makes it more possible for women to maintain their careers and care for their families. Let's keep our female talent and build the pipeline for women in leadership positions.

You don't have to be Cheryl Sandberg, a CEO, or even a C-suite executive to make a difference. Many of us wait until we have breached the glass ceiling before we start trying to help other women. Perhaps we don't believe we have the power to do it sooner. That's simply not true. In fact, we could create more power sooner if we banded together.

Stop treating your female colleagues like competitors. Instead, treat them like partners. Figure out what's worked for you in your own career and pass that knowledge onto another female. Reach out to a female peer who seems to be struggling or could be even better and more effective with a little advice. You don't have to tell her exactly what to do. You only need to share your own personal stories.

Consider mentoring a new female graduate or a young female professional to increase her odds of growing up to be a successful leader. Somebody, man or woman, took a chance on you. Someone invested discretionary time in you. You need to do the same: Take a chance on, and invest in, someone else. As an experienced female leader, you have the unique perspective on what it will take for that young woman to be successful. Don't keep it a secret. Share the knowledge that creates power and critical mass. Be a catalyst. That knowledge is like a fine piece of jewelry that doesn't do anyone any good hidden in the drawer. Get it out and share it with someone who will benefit from it.

These Ten Rules may sound like a lot to remember. But the message is simple. You will be a strong, impactful female leader if you make the effort to change a few behaviors. You will be more confident and courageous, and others will see you that way, too. You will build stronger relationships that will make you more influential. You will be visible and memorable. You will accomplish more. You will win more often. You will make a difference.

Most importantly, you will be happier because you will be more satisfied with your career, which directly affects your personal well-being. You don't need to change everything overnight. You do need to set your priorities, one at a time, and create a plan of action and then practice—every day.

12

GET ON WITH IT!

I CANNOT EMPHASIZE THE IMPORTANCE OF IMPLEMENT-
ing a strategy that will help attract and retain female talent
enough. You must keep this additional focus on female leaders until the changes you've made in culture, practices, policies, hiring, and promoting create sustainable results in your
organization. I urge you to not be patient about having more
gender balance. It's critical to getting the greatest possible
outcomes.

Generally, when a company needs resources to move its
business forward, the leaders go get them. There's no hesita-
tion about finding people who can add value to the business
or solve business problems. Yet in this case of getting more
women into leadership so that we have teams that are better,
and therefore organizations that are better, we are not only
hesitating, but we are also just not doing it!

If you are a male leader who, even after reviewing all of

the supporting evidence, is still skeptical, I urge you to ponder this question: What do you have to lose by giving this a shot and focusing on gender balance? What are you giving up by elevating your focus, building a great pipeline of talent, and increasing the diversity in leadership? It's not extra work. You build your employment brand, recruit for talent, build programs for employee engagement and retention, and invest in developing leaders anyway. All that's needed is to do these things differently. You may shift dollars and you may not, but you don't have to add any.

A change in your focus is not accommodation. It's not favoritism. You're not doing women a favor by making it easier for them to stay and lead; you're making your business better. If anything, these moves should be positioned as a strategy that is about improving the business rather than about making people happy.

Your business will be more interesting with more gender balance in leadership. There will be more engaging discussions about where the business is and where it's headed. The nature of the conversations will be more engrossing because the perspectives will vary more. Quite frankly, it will be more fun because you'll have more varied points of view, and though many executives won't openly admit it, they'd all prefer to work in an environment that is more fun.

What I've shared in the Ten Steps and the Ten Rules is not complicated. In fact, after reading them you might actually think it all sounds pretty simple. It is. There's not one action item that requires more people, more capital, more infrastructure, or more expense. When was the last time you were able to do something great for your business that didn't cost a cent?

What is not simple or easy is getting people to change the way they think and act. But it is achievable, and that is the key to the solution. We have to build new muscle memory. Everyone is capable of that. I'm sure you can recall more than one time in your career when you had to get the people around you to support a new strategy. This is no different. When a directive comes from a top leader giving people permission to think differently and presenting them with new ideas, they usually get on board. Those who don't shouldn't be allowed to stay.

The Ten Steps have to be driven from the top, starting with the CEO and his or her executive team. These leaders not only have to sponsor these initiatives, but they also must be involved. The initiatives will not work if there's only verbal support. Leaders must mentor, they must set examples, and they must understand the policies and practices and help develop new ones. They must own them.

One big caution: Don't start with the creation of a women's leadership initiative or affinity group. This is often the first step an executive team takes to demonstrate its commitment to developing and promoting women. Quite frankly, that's way down on the list of things you should do. Groups like that have been in existence for years. While they bring some benefit to the development of women leaders, there's no evidence that they actually make any impact in helping women get promoted. Women may learn from their peers and from guest speakers and will find those groups to be an additional support system; that's all good. But these efforts are not valuable without mentors, succession planning, leadership models, and practices that retain your female talent. Affinity groups should complement all of your other strategic initiatives to ensure more gender balance in leadership.

The Ten Steps are your road map. And while change will not happen overnight, you can see results in a fairly short period of time, beginning with improved morale, not just in the women in your organization but in everyone, particularly Millennials. They care about organizations doing the right things socially because they believe it's good for business. And because the availability of skilled workers in the United States will become more challenging over the next couple of decades, it's important that we pay attention to them now.

If you measure the rate of your turnover, then you can roughly predict when you will have opportunities to replace or promote the people in your organization. Whether you have female talent ready to step up or you have to hire from outside, it is precisely then that you have an opportunity to get more women in leadership.

Get your succession plan in order, and revisit it twice each year. You will be amazed at how quickly your organization actually changes, especially if you're driving changes instead of waiting for them to happen. Push to elevate high-potential workers and eliminate nonperformers. Make room to promote your top talent.

As for you women . . . you have got to take responsibility for driving change as well, altering your behaviors to raise your influence and leadership and helping other women do the same. There is power in numbers, and there is great power in raising other women's confidence. Revisit the Ten Rules periodically to truly own them.

I know that a lot of women who have heard me present the Ten Rules still have a difficult time introducing this subject in a way that generates any meaningful action. They are intimidated by initiating this conversation with their boss or colleagues, especially if those colleagues are men. More often, they take my materials to their human resource leaders (generally women), who contact me about coming and speaking to their organizations. That's not the answer.

I believe this book is the vehicle you need to start the conversation with the right leaders in your organization. That's why I wrote it. My suggestion is that you deliver this book to the leaders in your organization (particularly the male leaders) who can drive change. They are the ones you want to get the message, and they can help spread the message. And you'll be taking some of the steps that demonstrate your ability to lead.

The other suggestion I have for you is to leverage the forums you do have for women—by inviting the men. Bring a male boss or colleague. It doesn't even matter if they are from the same company or not. The goal is to get the men to hear and digest these messages and then, ultimately, take action.

Now is the time for all of us to get on with it. Enough talk. Let's start doing.

ACKNOWLEDGMENTS

NO ONE HAS EVER DESCRIBED ME AS BEING OUTWARDLY passionate about anything. More typically, I've been called thoughtful, logical, calm and steady but urgent, and determined. But as I began working on this book, I heard from the leaders I was interviewing, my friends, and my family: "It's clear you are really passionate about this." Suddenly, the passion is showing, most likely because I can already see the impact that talking, writing, and speaking about this topic is having on organizations and, particularly, female leaders.

I want to thank every leader who selflessly contributed time, experiences, and thoughts through my interviews. You are all smart, good people who run great organizations and are always striving to learn and be better. To the most important people in my life, my family, friends, and closest colleagues, particularly those who were forced to read my draft manuscripts and listen to my practice presentations over and over again (even my dog now understands this topic), a special thank you!

To my husband, David, thank you especially for the endless encouragement, support, and understanding of my "golf retirement" to pursue this project. To the leaders who participated in other ways, thank you. Whether you took part formally or through a casual conversation, I learned something from everyone. You all made the difference.

Trying to influence the world about the importance of having more gender balance in leadership is a huge task. But when you feel passionate about something, you have to make a start. The most significant changes in history started with individuals who spoke up, sometimes at the risk of their own lives. I can think of Rosa Parks, John F. Kennedy, Martin Luther King Jr., and Malala Yousafzai, to name a few. They started talking about something and kept talking about it, then talked about it some more. Don't get me wrong; I know this is not a life-threatening topic. The point is, when people drive the conversation and don't let it drop, eventually, someone pays attention, and they get others to pay attention, which eventually leads to critical mass. If you take away one thing that will affect change as a result of reading this book, then I will have succeeded in making a difference toward creating a sustainable strategic advantage.

Thanks to my supporters:

LORI A. BALL
President and Chief Operating Officer,
BioStorage Technologies, Inc.

ALLISON MARTIN-BOOKS
Chief Executive Officer, Diverse Talent Strategies

TORRENCE BOONE
Vice President, Global Sales and Service, Google

SUSAN W. BROOKS
Congresswoman, Indiana

JENIFER BROWN
Partner, Ice Miller LLP

KATHY CABELLO
President and Chief Executive Officer, Cabello Associates, Inc.

DAVID CAIN
President, Magnitude Agency

CHRISTOPHER CLAPP
Chief Executive Officer, Bluelock

ELLEN SWISHER CRABB
Vice Chairman, JBS United, Inc.

RICHARD P. CRYSTAL
Former Chairman and Chief Executive Officer,
New York & Company

TRACI DOLAN
Former Chief Administrative Officer, ExactTarget, Inc.

SCOTT DORSEY
Former Chief Executive Officer,
SalesForce ExactTarget Marketing Cloud

ANA DUTRA
President and Chief Executive Officer,
The Executives Club of Chicago

GAIL FARNSLEY
Executive Partner, Gartner,
and former Chief Information Officer, Cummins Inc.

KAREN FERGUSON FUSON
Group President, Gannett Community Publishing

MARY GANNON
Executive Vice President,
Edelman Media and Presentation Coaching

STEPHEN GOLDSMITH
    Daniel Paul Professor of Government,
    Harvard Kennedy School of Government

MINDY GROSSMAN
    Chief Executive Officer, HSN, Inc.

TIM HASSINGER
    President and Chief Executive Officer, Dow AgroSciences

ROB HILLMAN
    President, Anthem Blue Cross and Blue Shield, Indiana

J. MARK HOWELL
    Chief Operating Officer, Angie's List

STEVEN HUMKE
    Chief Managing Partner, Ice Miller LLP

DOLORES KUNDA
    Former President and Chief Executive Officer,
    Leo Burnett Puerto Rico

CATHY LANGHAM
    Owner and President, Langham Logistics, Inc.

LISA LUTHER
    Executive Vice President of Finance,
    HR and Business Operations, Nordstrom, Inc.

GLENN LYON
    Chairman and former Chief Executive Officer,
    The Finish Line, Inc.

JOE MAGNACCA
    Chief Executive Officer, Massage Envy,
    Former CEO, Radio Shack

BRYAN MILLS
    President and Chief Executive Officer,
    Community Health Network

PETER NORDSTROM
Co-President, Nordstrom, Inc.

JEN PETRO
Owner, DropLeaf Communications

PATTY PROSSER
Managing Partner, Career Consultants OI Partners

KATE QUINN
Executive Vice President,
Chief Strategy and Reputation Officer, US Bank

AMY RODGERS
Senior Vice President Human Resources,
Elite Comfort Solutions

SAMUEL SATO
Chief Executive Officer, The Finish Line, Inc.

KARL SCHOEMER
Owner and President, VisionQuest

ELLIOTT SIGAL
Former Chief Scientific Officer and Executive Vice President,
Bristol-Myers Squibb

MARY SPRINGER
Owner, That's Good HR Inc.

RANDALL TOBIAS
Former Chairman, President, and Chief Executive Officer,
Eli Lilly and Company, US Ambassador

JIM WEBER
Chairman and Chief Executive Officer,
Brooks Running Company

NICOLE WEBRE
CEO and Founder, Livewell Properties and Webre Consulting

DEANNA WISE

Executive Vice President and Chief Information Officer, Dignity Health

DAVID WORTMAN
Chairman and Chief Executive Officer, Diagnotes, Inc.

ENDNOTES

Prologue

1. Tony Schwartz, "What Women Know about Leadership That Men Don't," *Business Insider* 38 (August 2014), www.businessinsider.com/what-women-know-about-leadership-that-men-don't-2014-8

2. Sarah Childs and Mona Lena Krook, "Critical Mass Theory and Women's Political Representation," *Political Studies* 56 (2008): 725-736, doi: 10.1111/j.1467-9248.2007.00712.x

3. Aaron A. Dhir, *Challenging Boardroom Homogeneity: Corporate Law, Governance, and Diversity* (New York: Cambridge University Press, 2015).

4. Julia Dawson, Richard Kersley, and Stefano Natella, *The CS Gender 3000: Women in Senior Management* (Zurich: Credit Suisse Research Institute, 2014), https://publications.credit-suisse.com/tasks/render/file/index.cfm?fileid=8128F3C0-99BC-22E6-838E2A5B1E4366DF

Chapter Two

1. Anita Williams Woolley, Christopher F. Chabris, Alex Pentland, Nada Hashmi, and Thomas W. Malone, "Evidence for a Collective Intelligence Factor in the Performance of Human Groups," *Science* 29, no. 6004 (2010): 686-688, doi: 10.1126/science.1193147.

2. Mary Curtis, Christine Schmid, and Marion Struber, *Gender Diversity and Corporate Performance* (Zurich: Credit Suisse Research Institute, 2012), http://www.calstrs.com/sites/main/files/file-attachments/csri_gender_diversity_and_corporate_performance.pdf

3. Julia Dawson, Richard Kersley, and Stefano Natella, *The CS Gender 3000: Women in Senior Management* (Zurich: Credit Suisse Research Institute, 2014), https://publications.credit-suisse.com/tasks/render/file/index.cfm?fileid=8128F3C0-99BC-22E6-838E2A5B1E4366DF

4. Aaron A. Dhir, *Challenging Boardroom Homogeneity: Corporate Law, Governance, and Diversity* (New York: Cambridge University Press, 2015).

5. Chris Bart and Gregory McQueen, "Why Women Make Better Directors," *Int. J. Business Governance and Ethics* 8, no. 1, (2013): 93-99.

6. McKinsey & Company, "Gender Diversity in Top Management: Moving Corporate Culture, Moving Boundaries," (London: Women Matter 2013) November 2013.

7. Cathleen Benko and Molly Anderson, *The Corporate Lattice: Achieving High Performance in the Changing World of Work* (Boston: Harvard Business Review Press, 2013).

Chapter Four

1. Simon Baron-Cohen, *The Essential Difference: Male and Female Brains and the Truth about Autism.* (New York: Basic Books, 2003): 2121, 2150, 2151.

2. Katherine M. Bishop and Douglas Wahlsten, "Sex Differences in the Human Corpus Callosum: Myth or Reality," *Neuroscience and Biobehavioral Reviews* 21 (5): 581–601.

3. Madhura Ingalhalikar, Alex Smith, Drew Parker, Theodore D. Satterthwaite, Mark A. Elliott, Kosha Ruparel, Hakon Hakonarson, Raquel E. Gur, and Ragini Verma, "Sex Differences in the Structural Connectome of the Human Brain," Proceedings of the National Academy of Sciences 111 (2): 823–828, doi: 10.1073/pnas.1316909110.

Chapter Five

1. Anita Williams Woolley, Christopher F. Chabris, Alex Pentland, Nada Hashmi, and Thomas W. Malone, "Evidence for a Collective Intelligence Factor in the Performance of Human Groups," *Science* 29, no. 6004 (2010): 686-688, doi: 10.1126/science.1193147].
2. Caliper Research and Development Department, *Women Leaders Research Paper*, (Princeton: Caliper Whitepaper, December 2014), http://www.calipermedia.calipercorp.com.s3.amazonaws.com/whitepapers/us/Women-Leaders-2014.pdf

Chapter Six

1. Camille L. Ryan and Kurt Bauman, "Educational Attainment in the United States: 2015," *United States Census Bureau*, March 2016, http://www.census.gov/content/dam/Census/library/publications/2016/demo/p20-578.pdf
2. *The Bottom Line: Connecting Corporate Performance and Gender Diversity* (New York: Catalyst, 2004), http://www.catalyst.org/system/files/The_Bottom_Line_Connecting_Corporate_Performance_and_Gender_Diversity.pdf
3. Julia Dawson, Richard Kersley, and Stefano Natella, *The CS Gender 3000: Women in Senior Management* (Zurich: Credit Suisse Research Institute, 2014), https://publications.credit-suisse.com/tasks/render/file/index.cfm?fileid=8128F3C0-99BC-22E6-838E2A5B1E4366DF

4. Greg Pellegrino, Sally D'Amato, and Anne Weisberg, *The Gender Dividend: Making the Business Case for Investing in Women, Global Public Sector* (Deloitte, 2011), http://www.in.gov/icw/files/genderdividend.pdf

5. McKinsey & Company, (London: Women Matter 2013, 2013)

6. Julie Coffman and Bill Neuenfeldt, *Everyday Moments of Truth: Frontline Managers are Key to Women's Career Aspirations* (Bain & Company, June 17, 2014), http://www.bain.com/Images/BAIN_REPORT_Everyday_moments_of_truth.pdf.

7. The National Center for Education Statistics (NCES), *The Condition of Education* 2013, May 2013, NCES 2013-037.

8. National Women's Business Council (NWBC), "10 Million Strong: The Tipping Point for Women's Entrepreneurship: 2015 Annual Report," (Washington, DC: NWBC, 2015), www.nwbc.gov/sites/default/files/NWBC_2015AnnualReportedited.pdf

9. Dawson, Kersley, and Natella, *Gender 3000.*

Chapter Seven

1. National Science Board, *Science & Engineering Indicators 2016*, (Arlington, VA: National Science Foundation, 2016).

2. National Science Foundation, "Revisiting the STEM Workforce: A Companion to Science and Engineering Indicators 2014," (Arlington, VA: National Science Foundation, 2015).

3. The L'Oreal Foundation, "Women Three Times Less Likely than Men to Become Scientists, L'Oréal Foundation Finds," PR Newswire, March 19, 2014, www.prnewswire.com/news-release/women-three-times-less-likely-than-men-to-become-scientists-loreal-foundation-finds-250956171.html

4. Sylvia Ann Hewlett, Carolyn Buck Luce, Lisa J. Servon, Laura Sherbin, Peggy Shiller, Eytan Sosnovich, and Karen Sumberg, *The Athena Factor: Reversing the Brain Drain in Science, Engineering and Technology*, (Harvard Business Review Research Report, June 2008), http://documents.library.nsf.gov/edocs/

HD6060-.A84-2008-PDF-Athena-factor-Reversing-the-brain-drain-in-science,-engineering,-and-technology.pdf

5. National Science Foundation, "Women, Minorities and Persons with Disabilities in Science and Engineering Statistics 2015," *National Center for Science and Engineering Statistics* (2015), 15-311, http://www.nsf.gov/statistics/2015/nsf15311/start.cfm

6. National Science Board, op. cit.

7. Sylvia Ann Hewlett, Carolyn Buck Luce, Lisa J. Servon, Laura Sherbin, Peggy Shiller, Eytan Sosnovich, and Karen Sumberg, "The Athena Factor: Reversing the Brain Drain in Science, Engineering, and Technology," *Harvard Business Review* no. 10094, June 2008.

8. Christianne Corbett and Catherine Hill, "Solving the Equation: The Variables for Women's Success in Engineering and Computing," *AAUW*, March 2015, https://www.luminafoundation.org/files/resources/solving-the-equation.pdf

9. Corinne A. Moss-Racusin, John F. Dovidio, Victoria L. Brescoll, Mark J. Graham, and Jo Handelsman, "Science Faculty's Subtle Gender Biases Favor Male Students," *Proceedings of the National Academy of Sciences* 109, no. 41 (2012): 16474-16479, doi: 10.1073/pnas.1211286109.Harvard Business Review, op. cit.

10. Megan Smith, "Computer Science for All," The Whitehouse (blog), January 30, 2016, https://www.whitehouse.gov/blog/2016/01/30/computer-science-all

11. Deloitte, "Technology, Media, and Telecommunications Predictions 2016, (New York: Deloitte, 2016).

12. Janet Abbate, *Recoding Gender: Women's Changing Participation in Computing* (Cambridge, MA: The MIT Press, 2012).

13. *2015 Sales, Demographic and Usage Data: Essential Facts about The Computer and Video Game Industry*, (Entertainment Software Association, 2015), http://www.theesa.com/wp-content/uploads/2015/04/ESA-Essential-Facts-2015.pdf

14. Ann M Gallagher and James Kaufman, eds., *Gender Differences in Mathematics: An Integrative Psychological Approach* (New York: Cambridge University Press, 2005).

15. Moss-Racusin, op. cit.
16. Christianne Corbett and Catherine Hill, *Solving the Equation: The Variables for Women's Success in Engineering and Computing,* (Washington, DC: AAUW, 2015).
17. Ibid.
18. Gallagher and Kaufman (New York: Cambridge University Press, 2005).
19. Claudia Goldin, "Gender and the Undergraduate Economics Major: Notes on the Undergraduate Economics Major at a Highly Selective Liberal Arts College," *Scholars at Harvard,* last modified August 2013. http://scholar.harvard.edu/files/goldin/files/claudia_gender_paper.pdf?m=1429198526.
20. Ruth Schechter, "Malaysian Women Redefine Gender Roles in Technology," Stanford University, The Clayman Institute for Gender Research, February 8, 2010, http://gender.stanford.edu/news/2011/malaysian-women-redefine-gender-roles-technology http://scholar.harvard.edu/files/goldin/files/claudia_gender_paper.pdf?m=1429198526
21. Sylvia Ann Hewlett, Carolyn Buck Luce, Lisa J. Servon, Laura Sherbin, Peggy Shiller, Eytan Sosnovich, and Karen Sumberg, "The Athena Factor: Reversing the Brain Drain in Science, Engineering, and Technology," *Harvard Business Review* no. 10094, June 2008.
22. Ibid.
23. Susan Adams, "10 Great Companies for Women in 2015," *Forbes/Leadership*, March 2015, http://www.forbes.com/sites/susanadams/2015/03/03/ten-great-companies-for-women-in-2015/#295d9e41501e
24. Ibid.

Chapter Eight

1. Richard Dobbs, Anu Madgavkar, Dominic Barton, Eric Labaye, James Manyika, Charles Roxburgh, Susan Lund, and Siddarth Madhav, *The World at Work: Jobs, Pay, and Skills for 3.5 Billion People* (McKinsey Global Institute, June 2012).

2. Jared Council, "Research Shows Benefit of Women in Startup Management Teams," *Indiana Business Journal*, October 17, 2015, http://www.ibj.com/articles/55357-research-shows-benefit-of-women-in-startup-management-teams

Chapter Nine

1. McKinsey & Company, (Women Matter 2013, 2013).

2. Boris Groysberg and Katherine Connolly, "Great Leaders Who Make the Mix Work," *Harvard Business Review*, September 2013, hbr.org/2013/09/great-leaders-who-make-the-mix-work

Chapter Ten

1. Boris Groysberg and Deborah Bell, "2012 Board of Directors Survey," (Chicago: Heidrick & Struggles and Women Corporate Directors, 2012): www.heidrick.com//media/Publications%20and%20Reports/WCD_2012BoardSurvey.pdf

2. Julia Dawson, Richard Kersley, and Stefano Natella, *The CS Gender 3000: Women in Senior Management* (Zurich: Credit Suisse Research Institute, 2014), https://publications.credit-suisse.com/tasks/render/file/index.cfm?fileid=8128F3C0-99BC-22E6-838E2A5B1E4366DF

3. Tara Sophia Mohr, "Why Women Don't Apply for Jobs Until They're 100% Qualified," *Harvard Business Review*, August 25, 2014, https://hbr.org/2014/08/why-women-dont-apply-for-jobs-unless-theyre-100-qualified

Chapter Eleven

1. Catherine G. Krupnick, "Women and Men in the Classroom: Inequality and Its Remedies," *On Teaching and Learning*, vol. 1 (1985).
2. "Female Politicians Inspire Women in India To Pursue More Education, MIT Study Finds," *Huffpost Women*, January 18, 2012, http://www.huffingtonpost.com/2012/01/18/mit-study-india-female-leaders-politicians-aspirations_n_1213998.html

AUTHOR Q & A

▲

Q: You express that it took some time before you realized that the progress of getting more women in leadership was not moving as fast as it should. Was there something that happened to bring this issue to mind? How did this realization affect you as a leader?

A: After executive leaders like Sheryl Sandberg and Sallie Krawcheck, as well as others, started bringing more attention and press to the challenge, I became more involved with initiatives designed to provide mentoring to women. It was through those conversations that I began to realize what the barriers were for women. I was curious enough to not only ask for women's perspectives but I also asked many male executive leaders what they thought was getting in the way. As an executive leader myself, I felt a certain responsibility to collect these opinions and offer solutions to the problem. I've seen how the strategies I'm recommending help organizations succeed in being more productive and successful. These strategies are simple and they work! As a female leader, I also wanted to provide useful advice to women to help them. The advice I'm sharing has helped many women push their careers forward.

Q: As a woman in a leadership role, what are some of the struggles you faced to get there? Do you feel it was harder for you to achieve success than it was for men in the same kinds of roles?

A: I was fortunate to have great mentors and supporters along the path of my career. I don't feel that it was harder for me than it was for men to be successful. In fact, I was just as successful as the men and my teams appreciated my leadership style because it was different. I always got results, but I got them differently. That doesn't mean I didn't feel the challenges of being the only woman in the room. I accepted that and dealt with it. I believe it would have been less challenging at times to be heard if there had been more people in the room who were wired like me. As I state in the book, having critical mass is important.

In general, I've seen women struggle more with balancing a leadership role and managing a family. Because women have been the primary caregivers, for them, it meant pulling work out late in the evening after children were in bed. I saw how, for these women, that way of life resulted in exhaustion, which then often resulted in difficult personal dilemmas. Women (or men) should not have to choose between having a family and making a living.

Q: What would your advice be to men who wish to make a positive impact on gender-balanced leadership? What is your advice to women who wish to make a positive impact on gender-balanced leadership?

A: My advice to men is to take some deliberate steps to make this happen. It really won't happen otherwise. Take this on the same way you do other business challenges. Map out a plan, take action, measure and communicate results. For women in leadership, you are in a unique position to help other women. Do it. Mentor and sponsor others. For you, it's mostly about helping other women change their behaviors as you did.

Q: *Money on the Table* is an interesting title for your book, and it touches on your belief that businesses can benefit monetarily from gender equality. Can you explain how gender-balanced leadership can help businesses profit?

A: As I explain in this book, men and women are wired differently. We think differently, problem-solve, and communicate differently. These differences mean varied perspectives. More varied perspectives mean better ideas and solutions. Better solutions mean better products and services. Continuous evolution of products and services is required to remain competitive, regardless of what industry you're competing in.

Q: Can you give us some insight into the ways in which businesses and executives have been willing or unwilling to accept and relate to women in leadership positions?

A: I don't believe it's an issue of willingness or unwillingness. It's more about understanding that there are different ways of thinking that are inherent to women and men, and learning how to leverage those differences. It's also about understanding and accepting that women want to work for different reasons. Women think harder about the value they can add versus the title they can get. They think more about how the work will impact self-satisfaction and how it will affect their personal lives. If we're going to have the best talent, we all have to learn how to appeal to these needs and desires, which, in turn, will provide a return to our businesses.

Q: Has there been any particular woman in leadership who has been an influence or a source of inspiration in your life? How has this person helped shape your ideas, your goals and visions, and your beliefs about gender equality in leadership?
A: I'm not able to call out one particular woman in leadership who was a source of inspiration, because I have learned valuable lessons from many. To be honest, the women who have had the most impact on my beliefs are the highly talented ones who left companies and careers because they couldn't excel in their environments. They gave up. Those losses have been my true inspiration to drive change.

Q: You talk about the similarities between Millennials and women in the workforce and how these two groups are no longer driven primarily by money. Money is important, but they are really looking for more balance in their lives. How did you first recognize these similarities? How do you think this shift in priorities will affect the future of business and business leadership?

A: When it comes to money, women and Millenials are driven by fairness. They want to be paid what is competitive. *After* that, money is not generally the top priority. Doing meaningful work and having a meaningful life outside of work are the priorities. This shift in priorities means leaders now have to figure out how they can structure work that supports both the growth of the business and the growth of people. You really can't do one successfully without doing the other.

Q: What do you see as the most important thing that businesses and other organizations can do to ensure that future generations of women, like yourself, can have a "seat at the table?"

A: The answer to this is simple. We must be deliberate in the choices we make about who we're hiring, grooming, and promoting for leadership positions. We have to stop being afraid of talking about how we'll consider gender balance in making these decisions. Gender is not the only factor that should be considered, but too often it's not being considered at all.

Q: Finally, if you could name the single most significant concept or piece of information you hope your readers will take away after reading *Money on the Table*, what would it be and why?

A: I'll go back to the takeaways in the prologue. As a leader, you're leaving money on the table if you don't have women well represented on your boards and leadership teams. The hardwiring of both women and men is necessary to have the best thinking, communication, and problem-solving to have the best products and services for your customers. You have to change practices that will get more gender balance in leadership, and you need to do that with urgency.

ABOUT THE AUTHOR

▲

MELISSA GREENWELL IS EXECUTIVE VICE PRESIDENT and chief operating officer for national retailer The Finish Line, Inc. She has had an extensive career as a C-suite executive and trusted advisor with a "seat at the table." And yes, most of those tables were filled with men, so she knows what she's talking about. Previously, Greenwell held the position of chief human resources officer at Finish Line. She is an excellent example of a female senior leader who stepped out of the boundaries of a support role into an operations role that is key to driving revenue for a public company. She has spent her career partnering with executive teams to create people strategies that support business objectives in organization design, performance and rewards, succession planning, leadership development, and employee engagement.

Greenwell is also a certified executive coach who helps women and men understand how they can leverage natural strengths to identify and make behavioral changes that help them succeed as senior leaders. Helping leaders understand how they can affect and leverage the perceptions they create to get others to follow is central to her model.

Greenwell has received numerous awards and recognitions for executive and community leadership. Beyond developing high-potential leaders, she shares her time with several not-for-profit organizations, including those focused on developing aspiring female leaders.